LLEWELLYN'S
CLASSIC
TAROT
COMPANION

LLEWELLYN'S
CLASSIC
TAROT
COMPANION

CREATED BY
BARBARA MOORE

ILLUSTRATED BY
EUGENE SMITH

Llewellyn Publications
Woodbury, Minnesota

FIRST EDITION
First Printing, 2014

Book design by Rebecca Zins
Cover design by Lisa Novak
Illustrations © 2014 by Eugene Smith
Interior floral ornaments from *1500 Decorative Ornaments* (Dover Publications, 2000)

Llewellyn is a registered trademark of Llewellyn Worldwide Ltd.

ISBN 978-0-7387-3608-2
Llewellyn's Classic Tarot kit consists of a boxed set of 78 full-color cards and this perfect-bound book.

Llewellyn Publications
A Division of Llewellyn Worldwide Ltd.
2143 Wooddale Drive
Woodbury, MN 55125-2989
www.llewellyn.com

Printed in the United States of America

CONTENTS

INTRODUCTION

L lewellyn's Classic Tarot was designed to be faithful to the traditional tarot images, symbols, and meanings recognizable to most modern tarot readers and students. Creating a faithful yet new expression of timeless tarot imagery is quite a challenge. Like the masters of Chinese tea ceremonies who find ways to express their uniqueness creatively within the strict confines of the tea ritual, we had to discover our voice within the structure of traditional tarot.

Because this deck is based firmly on the foundation of modern tarot, this book also focuses on classic interpretation. The first chapter provides an introduction to tarot and its history, techniques for learning and practicing tarot reading, and a survey of important facets of tarot interpretation and reading such as correspondences and reversals. The next three chapters present the card interpretations, including keywords, symbolism, and reversed meanings. Chapter 5 explains how to do a reading and provides several spreads to use.

Tarot has fascinated people for hundreds of years. It is particularly useful for divination, whether you are divining possible future events or seeking understanding and guidance. This is because it helps bring us to a place where insight is supported. Tarot does this by engaging both parts of the human mind, the logical and the intuitive. The structure of tarot is recognized by our logic, and the images stimulate our intuition. By using a tool that lets both parts of our brain shine, we can more easily access our best selves. When we are at our best, it is easier to clearly see our way forward.

Tarot is a wonderful world, one that many people spend their entire lives exploring. If you are new to tarot, we hope that this set gives you a firm foundation for your own journey. If you are a seasoned tarot reader, we hope that these cards become one of your most useful and easy-to-read decks.

CHAPTER 1

TAROT BASICS

Before exploring the individual card meanings, it is helpful to have an overview of the deck and of some characteristics of reading the cards. This chapter provides a roadmap of a typical tarot deck and will help as you begin your journey through each individual card.

Key Terms

Arcana: secrets

Court Cards: sixteen cards, four from each suit, usually named page, knight, queen, and king

Major Arcana: twenty-two cards that are named and numbered

Minor Arcana: fifty-six cards that are divided into four suits—Wands, Cups, Swords, and Pentacles—each with ten pips and four court cards

Pips: forty cards, ten in each suit, numbered ace through ten

Querent: the person who the reading is for; the person asking the question

Reader: the person reading, or interpreting, the cards

Reversal or Reversed Card: a card that appears upside-down relative to the reader

Spread: a diagram showing how to lay out the cards and describing what each position signifies

Characteristics of a Tarot Deck

A tarot deck is a pack of seventy-eight cards with a specific structure, comprised of two main sections called the Major Arcana and the Minor Arcana. *Arcana* means "secret." The Minor Arcana, with fifty-six cards, is very similar to a pack of playing cards. There are four suits: Wands, Cups, Swords, and Pentacles. Each suit includes an ace through ten plus four court cards: page, knight, queen, and king. The Major Arcana, with twenty-two cards, is a little different. The cards are numbered zero through twenty-one. There is no other external structure in this section. Each card bears a title such as the Empress, the Wheel of Fortune, or the Moon. The Minor Arcana represents the people, places, and events of everyday life, while the Major Arcana represents larger themes, milestones, and life-changing events. Both groups of cards work together, when shuffled and laid out in a reading, to create snapshots of the human experience.

The name *tarot* is given to most any deck that follows this structure, although there are decks that claim the name with additional cards or even extra suits. Whether the inclusion of these extras means they are not true tarot decks is open for debate. Some maintain that a tarot deck is defined by this structure and that if a deck deviates from it, then it is no longer a tarot deck. Others say that tarot is organic and that since it has changed from the earliest decks to what we now consider "traditional," it is in the nature of tarot to evolve. For those who see tarot as a reflection of and a tool for spiritual exploration and growth, then it makes sense to say that tarot would evolve to reflect humanity's evolving spiritual understanding.

The deck explored in this book was designed to be very traditional. It is based on the Rider-Waite-Smith (RWS) deck designed by Arthur E. Waite, drawn by Pamela Colman Smith, and published by the Rider Company in 1910. The RWS deck was not the first tarot deck ever published, but it is the one that changed the course of tarot history and exerted the greatest influence on modern tarot readers, particularly in the United States. We will learn more about this deck in the next section. To understand tarot, it is important to know its history—both of the cards themselves and the way people have used the cards.

A Brief History

Tarot, as far as we know, was invented during the Renaissance. The cards were hand-painted and often adorned with gold leaf. They were miniature works of art that were sometimes commissioned as gifts. We know, for example, that in the mid-fifteenth century a deck was commissioned to celebrate the marriage of Francesco Sforza and Bianca Maria Visconti.

Although today tarot cards are used by some to tell the future, in the fifteenth century they were used to play a card game that involved trick-taking, like bridge or euchre. In fact, in some parts of Europe it is still a popular game that is played with decks of tarot cards purchased at tobacco shops.

While there is some evidence that tarot and playing cards were used to tell fortunes in the sixteenth century, it wasn't until the eighteenth century that tarot became fully immersed in the esoteric world. A pastor named Antoine Court de Gébelin was the first that we know of to claim an occult connection with the cards. He associated a card with a letter of the Hebrew alphabet, and thus the connection between tarot and Qabalah was born. Later, a Parisian seed salesman, Jean-Baptiste Alliette (who wrote under the name Etteilla, which is "Alliette" spelled backwards) created the first deck specifically for divination, but it was quite different from existing tarot decks before or since.

In the nineteenth century secret societies abounded, and through them tarot was connected with all sorts of things such as alchemy, Qabalah, and astrology. In 1909, Golden Dawn member Alfred E. Waite published his deck through the Rider Company, with images painted by Pamela (Pixie) Colman Smith. Now known as the Rider-Waite Tarot or Rider-Waite-Smith Tarot, it is one of the most important decks ever created. In 1943, Aleister Crowley and artist Lady Frieda Harris completed the Thoth Tarot, which wasn't published until 1969 and is still popular with readers today. However, for whatever reason, the Rider-Waite-Smith Tarot has become the standard, particularly in the United States. Most beginners learn with this deck, and a majority of decks published today are based on the RWS tradition even though it was not the first tarot deck ever designed or even the first designed for divination.

In the early twentieth century, tarot was primarily used in two ways. The fortuneteller approach was common and gave rise to some popular Hollywood ideas about tarot readers, including proclamations about tall, dark strangers, perilous journeys over water, and sudden death. The secret societies used the cards as placeholders for esoteric knowledge and spiritual belief systems. Using the cards in this way has shaped the modern tarot practice of correspondences, which we'll discuss below.

After the start of World War I, interest in tarot waned. That waning interest reignited in the 1960s. Eden Gray's *The Tarot Revealed* and *Mastering the Tarot* were published, inspiring a new generation of tarot enthusiasts. Gray's work was an amalgamation of fortuneteller meanings and secret society practices. In the 1970s, people who learned from Gray went on to change tarot in a way that affects the way that readers, students, and authors view tarot even today. In fact, by the mid-1980s two women published works that have probably been among the most-loved tarot books of the last thirty years. Rachel Pollack published her two-volume *78 Degrees of Wisdom*, an in-depth study of card meanings weaving together esotericism, mythology, and psychology. Mary K. Greer published *Tarot for Your Self*, which teaches how to read the cards for personal insight and psychological transformation.

From a game to secret occult teachings to mystical stereo-types to psychology, tarot has played many roles. Societies and individuals have looked into the mirror that is tarot, and the reflections revealed changes both in cultures and individuals. Tarot, sometimes called the Royal Road, has followed a path rich in entertainment, mystery, wisdom, and beauty through the years. And each of us who ever shuffles a deck takes part in that ongoing journey, shaping it and being shaped by it.

If you are interested in learning more about tarot history, consult Robert M. Place's *The Fool's Journey: The History, Art & Symbolism of the Tarot*.

Correspondences

There are many reasons why tarot is so popular. One is that for people who love to study and learn new things, with tarot there is always more to explore. In addition to learning about the cards themselves, reading practices, and other tarot-centric activities, tarot is a springboard and a bridge for learning other seemingly non-tarot-related topics. The structure of a tarot deck lends itself so easily to so many modalities, such as astrology, numerology, or Qabalah. Connecting the tarot to other subjects or other ways of looking at the world has led to elaborate tables of correspondences.

The cards, either individually or in groups/suits, have been associated with many, many things over the years; for example: astrological signs, planets, seasons, numerology, Myers-Briggs personality types, Hebrew letters, Sephiroth, paths on the Tree of Life, colors, alchemy, musical notes, runes, plants, stones, directions, I Ching, and socio-economic divisions.

In addition to all those associations (and more), different schools of thought sometimes assign the correspondences differently. There are no absolutes. As long as the connection makes sense and meshes with your philosophy, then that is the right one for you.

Learning and using correspondences is not required in order to read the cards or even to deeply understand them. The only exception is the elemental associations, as they are so integral to understanding the suits; fortunately, the elements—fire, water, air, and earth—are quite intuitive. Using any other correspondences should only enhance your understanding or add to your enjoyment of studying the cards or aid in learning the subject being associated.

Astrological, elemental, and Qabalastic associations are the most common. However, if you know nothing of astrology, reading that the Fool corresponds to Uranus doesn't deepen or expand your understanding the card and can cause frustration. Knowing that Binah is associated with the threes and the queens is helpful to someone who is familiar with the Tree of Life but merely bewildering to someone who has never heard of the Tree of Life.

It is not necessary to learn astrology or Qabalah to learn tarot. However, if you already know these subjects, seeing how they correspond will make learning the cards easier. It works the other way, too. Once you know tarot, if you want to learn astrology, knowing the astrological correspondences to tarot will create a bridge and help you learn more quickly.

Correspondences are just one of the things that make tarot a fascinating, life-long study. It is also sometimes a source of frustration. While tarot does lend itself to other modalities, none fit absolutely and perfectly. Many times some of the connections seem to make sense with the card's meaning and image and other times the assigned correspondence seems to contradict the meaning or, worse, have no apparent connection at all. For people who enjoy studying and talking about tarot, this is not a problem; it only adds to the fun and interest.

The most commonly used correspondences for the individual cards, suits, and ranks are listed in this book in the appropriate sections. If they enhance your understanding of the card, use them. If not, save them for later and explore their connections to what you know about cards.

Reversals

When you shuffle and lay out your cards, you may notice that some may be oriented upside down—that is, the top of the card will be at the bottom. These are called reversed cards or reversals. Not all readers incorporate reversals. Some will carefully shuffle so that no reversals occur or simply reorient the card so that they are all right-side up.

Because this book is committed to presenting traditional material, common reversed meanings are included. However, many modern readers feel that the old reversed meanings are arbitrary and therefore opt not use them at all. You should try both methods and decide for yourself.

Other modern readers use reversals but use a system rather than traditional meanings. Instead of individual reversed card meanings, they assign a general meaning that influences the reversed card. Here are some examples:

- All reversed cards mean the opposite of their upright meaning.
- All reversed cards indicate that the energy of that card is blocked, repressed, or denied.
- All reversed cards are read as an inner or unconscious experience.
- All reversed cards are the negative extreme of the upright meaning.

If you are curious about reversals, consult Mary K. Greer's *Complete Book of Tarot Reversals*.

Now that you have an overview of what to expect, it's time to explore each card in depth.

CHAPTER 2

THE MAJOR ARCANA

The cards of the Major Arcana are often considered the most important in the deck, with good reason, since they are the "major" secrets. They represent significant life events, milestones, and turning points. They often indicate spiritual or life-changing energy and frequently signify experiences that are beyond the querent's control.

O • THE FOOL

The Fool

Keywords: beginnings, innocence, freedom, spontaneity, adventure, youth, idealism, faith, purity, fearlessness, carelessness, eccentricity, apparent foolishness

Reversed: folly, foolishness, carelessness, stupidity, negligence, distraction, naivety, recklessness, risk-taking

Astrological: Uranus

Element: air

Symbols:

white dog: inner voice, distractions

sun: joy, optimism

stick with bag: lessons from previous lives, innate abilities

red feather in cap: passion, heart

white rose: purity

cliff: leap of faith

brightly colored clothing: unique, careless, or eccentric nature

A bright sun bathes the scene in joy and optimism. The Fool steps forth with eyes closed, as if following inner guidance. The dog alerts him to the potential danger of the cliff or perhaps distracts him from his path. While aware, at least on some level, of the danger, the Fool walks in faith, confidently following his dreams. Passion guides the head, and purity of purpose leads the way.

The Fool represents the start of a new journey or phase of life, one that may seem foolish but also brings a sense of freedom. There is no plan, perhaps not even a clear goal, just an intense drive to take the leap. The small bag indicates that the decision is rather spontaneous. Only what is essential is taken; everything else is left behind.

The Magician

Keywords: will, talent, skill, creativity, manifestation, communication, magic, action, awareness, power, resourcefulness, concentration, eloquence

Reversed: trickery, manipulation, deceit, con, liar, misuse of gifts

Astrological: Mercury

Element: air

Symbols:

red roses: passion

white lilies: purity

sword, cup, wand, and pentacle on table: the four suits of tarot

right arm up, left arm down: as above, so below

lemniscate: infinite flow of energy

ouroboros: eternity, transformation

red and white clothing: passion and purity

wand in right hand: will

The Magician functions under a fundamental belief: as above, so below. This means that the higher plane of existence is reflected in the lower plane. Using his understanding of the laws of the universe as well as any tools and resources at his disposal, he can achieve his goals. Essentially, this is making magic: working with energy to create change in the world. With the right balance of passion and purity, he can achieve almost anything. He is no dabbler, though. He wields his will with wisdom gained through study and experience.

I · THE MAGICIAN

He knows that the strongest magic he can ever work is his own transformation.

The Magician represents having the knowledge, skill, and resources to manifest one's will. With this power comes responsibility.

II · THE HIGH PRIESTESS

The High Priestess

Keywords: secrets, initiation, mystery, silence, wisdom, understanding, intuition, insight, subconscious, unrevealed future

Reversed: shallow knowledge, secrets, hidden agendas, passion, conceit

Astrological: Moon

Element: water

Symbols:

black and white pillars: entry between light and dark

B and J on columns: Boaz and Jachin, marking the entrance to the Temple of Solomon

tapestry with pomegranate tree: life blood, feminine secrets, Persephone's journey to the underworld

rolled-up scroll: secrets, knowledge that is experienced rather than taught

equal-armed cross: the meeting of spiritual and material worlds

triple goddess headpiece: the moon and its mysteries, cycles, changeable nature, subconscious

crescent moon: the moon and its mysteries, cycles, changeable nature, subconscious

dress becoming river: the future is ever changing

The High Priestess guards the threshold of an initiation. An initiation provides knowledge, insight, or wisdom that cannot be taught; it can only be gained through direct experience. Because she does not share this information, this card represents something that cannot be revealed at this time. The High Priestess is connected with water, indicating her ability to understand the flow of the ever-changing future. Consequently there is no clear answer, since the future is still being formed.

The High Priestess represents a time of not knowing outcomes and not receiving clear answers. Some things are not in our best interest to know ahead of time. Go through the experience knowing that you will gain important wisdom through doing so. This initiatory time is a test of your knowledge to date, and your actions during this time will strongly shape the future.

The Empress

Keywords: abundance, fertility, creativity, pleasure, beauty, happiness, comfort, nature, motherhood, mother, nurturing, love, pregnancy, generosity

Reversed: dependence, codependence, laziness, stagnation, smothering, stubbornness, creative block, gluttony

Astrological: Venus

Element: earth

Symbols:

lush garden: fertility, abundance

wheat: nurturing, abundance

Venus glyph: love, values, feminine energy

white gown with pomegranates: purity, passion, love, fertility

twelve-starred crown: Queen of the Heavens, cycles of time

The Empress reigns over nature in the comfort of her luxurious throne. The stars on her crown represent the role of time and cycles in the circle of life. She is nature, life, and growth. She is also the whole process from birth to ripening to death. She is abundance, which is not merely enough but more than enough. She nourishes but also provides a beautiful feast for the senses. She is the enjoyment and sharing of all good things.

The Empress represents the garden of life and the role of the gardener. We take care of the land, enrich the soil, select

III · THE EMPRESS

the seeds, care for the seedlings, water, weed, and harvest. She marks a time of fecundity and possibility. She promises rich soil, but the responsibility of planting, caring for, and harvesting the fruits of our lives is ours.

IV • THE EMPEROR

The Emperor

Keywords: stability, structure, power, authority, leadership, control, protection, stewardship, order, leadership, boss, fatherhood, father, ambition, reason, logic, confidence

Reversed: tyranny, rigidity, inflexibility, controlling, cruelty, abuse of power, poor leadership, undisciplined

Astrological: Aries

Element: fire

Symbols:

rams' heads: association with Aries

armor and red tunic: the will to defend and protect

cube-like throne: structure, stability

red and white jewels in crown: pure and passionate leadership

orb and wand: balancing the needs of society with the resources available

If the Empress is the creator of resources, the Emperor manages those resources for the greater good, focusing on order, efficiency, prosperity, and stability. He surveys the entire situation and makes decisions accordingly. While he does wield much power, he is aware of the responsibility that always rests on his shoulders. His role is not merely to impose his will but to create order in a way that benefits the larger picture.

The Emperor represents the role that authority, power, and responsibility play in our lives. Structures of society shape daily life, sometimes in positive ways and sometimes in challenging or oppressive ways. People also create structure in their own lives, managing their resources and reaping the consequences, for better or worse, of their decisions.

The Hierophant

Keywords: education, teaching, learning, knowledge, conformity, tradition, institutions, group identity, values, guidance, orthodoxy, rites, blessing, status quo, social conventions

Reversed: fundamentalism, repression, intolerance, fear, guilt, extremism, restriction, cults, abuse of position

Astrological: Taurus

Element: earth

Symbols:

two pillars: path between heaven and earth

acolytes: teaching and learning

crossed keys: keys to understanding both theory and practice

papal garb and crown: spiritual authority

hand gesture: blessing, higher ideals shaping earthly experience

The Hierophant's title comes from the word *hierophany,* meaning "the manifestation of the sacred." A hierophant teaches us how to express lofty beliefs and spiritual aspirations in everyday life. He focuses on teaching and instruction. His goal is not about following the rules of a demanding and illogical deity but rather about bringing faith to life and manifesting the sacred in this world.

The Hierophant represents our relationship with our faith or guiding principles and how we choose to deepen

V · THE HIEROPHANT

our understanding and express those beliefs through our thoughts, feelings, and actions. Part of this includes balancing individual needs with that of the larger community. Symbolically this card focuses on spiritual knowledge, but it can also represent any kind of formal education.

VI · THE LOVERS

The Lovers

Keywords: choices, crossroads, trust, communication, relationships, partnerships, togetherness, love, affection, sexuality, harmony, engagement, attraction, duality

Reversed: separation, disharmony, suspicion, jealousy, obsession, infidelity, fear of commitment, loss of love

Astrological: Gemini

Element: air

Symbols:

woman: feminine, intuitive nature

man: masculine, logical nature

nudity: nothing hidden

apple tree: knowledge of good and evil, choices

snake: temptation

leaves of fire: passion and will

Raphael: archangel, healing power of God and love

sun: knowledge, clarity

In addition to its connotations of romantic love, the Lovers is also about the union of opposites, communion with the Divine, and completion. In either case, it is really about making a choice.

More specifically, it is about making the right choice in a situation where both options hold strong appeal. Archangel Raphael suggests that the best answer is the one that promises love and healing.

The Lovers represents an important decision to be made. Exercising free will is a way of creating the future. It will be important to choose wisely. Relying on both the heart and head, being honest with one's self, and recognizing the difference between temptation and viable option should make the task simpler.

The Chariot

Keywords: drive, ambition, control, direction, determination, success, triumph, victory, will, movement, progress, speed, travel, conquest, battle

Reversed: lack of control, delay, opposition, stagnation, no direction, aggression, canceled trip, car trouble

Astrological: Cancer

Element: water

Symbols:

The Chariot includes symbols from cards I through VI, showing the integration of the lessons of those cards.

starry canopy: Empress's starry crown

wand: Magician's wand

lingam and yoni: the union of the Lovers

square shape of the chariot: Emperor

black and white sphinxes: High Priestess's pillars and also the Hierophant standing above his acolytes

crescent moon: High Priestess

Without the benefit of reins, the Chariot must rely on his will alone to urge the two sphinxes forward. As is the wont of sphinxes, he must answer a riddle to proceed. In this case, the riddle involves knowledge of the previous six cards. Until then, the desire to move forward is impeded. The impasse is usually based in a conflict of some sort, as shown by the sphinxes. Does he really want to give up the life he has known and move forward into the unknown?

VII · THE CHARIOT

The Chariot represents a time for taking control of one's life, of using all the knowledge gained over a lifetime to make the choice and move forward. The intuition of the High Priestess, the love of the Empress, the rationality of the Emperor, the training of the Hierophant, and the passion of the Lovers come together to fuel the ride. But it is the will of the Magician that makes it all work together, causing the spark that starts the forward motion.

VIII · Strength

Strength

Keywords: strength, gentleness, patience, compassion, healing, integration, courage, heart, control, discipline, fortitude, assurance, potency, virility, lust, instinct, ability, mastery

Reversed: weakness, overbearing, force, cowardice, fear, shyness; lack of discipline, control, or patience

Astrological: Leo

Element: fire

Symbols:

white gown: purity

woman: virtue, feminine energy

lion: animal instincts, fears, ego, shadow

red roses: desire

lemniscate: infinite flow of energy

A serene, calm, gentle-looking woman in white places her hands on top of and under the mouth of a lion, as if closing its mouth. The lion could easily take her down, yet it is submitting to her gentle pressure. She is taming it with calm compassion, not controlling it through brute force.

The lion represents any part of one's self that threatens to overtake one. It can be excess ego, base desires, or the shadow self. Repressing these aspects works for a time but always fails in the end. Through understanding and integration, the power of these aspects becomes part of the infinite flow, as indicated by the lemniscate.

Strength represents facing fears with courage and compassion. Facing fears with fear makes a bad situation worse, while a pure and brave heart can transform the situation. The ability to change something from bad to good is true strength.

The Hermit

Keywords: solitude, introspection, philosophy, meditation, withdrawal, contemplation, wisdom, guidance, seeking, mysticism, privacy, prudence

Reversed: introversion, agoraphobia, ostracism, exile, paranoia, loneliness, isolation, extreme withdrawal, self-absorption, social misfit

Astrological: Virgo

Element: earth

Symbols:

dark cloak: mystery, isolation

staff: will, accumulated knowledge

lantern: inner guidance, inner divinity

six-pointed star: union of water and fire

mountaintop: journey, "big picture" point of view

winter: old age, experience, wisdom

The Hermit walks his own path, supported by the wisdom he has gathered over the years, symbolized by his strong, tall staff. But the main focus here is the light he carries. More than anything else, his own inner divine spark guides him. He follows no one and does not care if anyone follows him.

The Hermit represents a time of no longer listening to others or seeking guidance from anyone else. It is time to withdraw and weigh all the information gathered against the only measure that matters: one's own truth. Being alone and removing all other influences is the best avenue to self-discovery. In this way, one's light shines in the darkness and grows

THE MAJOR ARCANA

IX · THE HERMIT

stronger. It may be that such a light attracts others, but that is not what is important. Anyone's light can be an example, but in the end, we must all light our own way.

THE MAJOR ARCANA

X · THE WHEEL OF FORTUNE

The Wheel of Fortune

Keywords: fortune, chance, cycle of life, opportunity, destiny, fate, good luck, movement, turning point, annual event

Reversed: bad luck, out of control, misfortune, failure, unexpected setback, reversal, delay

Astrological: Jupiter

Element: fire

Symbols:

The four fixed signs of the zodiac:

- Angel = Aquarius
- Eagle = Scorpio
- Lion = Lion
- Bull = Taurus

The four alchemical symbols of the substances required for alchemical transformation:

- North = mercury
- East = sulfur
- South = water
- West = salt

English letters (T, A, R, O): rota (Latin for "wheel"), taro (tarot), orat (Latin for "speaks"), tora (Hebrew law), Ator (Egyptian goddess of love)

Hebrew letters: Tetragrammaton, the most powerful name of God

The Egyptian gods on the wheel:

- Sphinx and the sword of truth at the top: while not always obvious, life is always governed by the laws of truth and the universe
- Anubis: guides dead souls to new life
- Typhon: the destruction of death

We face a game of chance, a strange wheel covered in riddles and cloaked in mystery. The only constant is change. We may assume that the Wheel of Fortune turns in a slow, natural progression, but that would be a mistake. Perhaps the Wheel of Life does that, but Fortune is a bit more unpredictable. The Wheel of Fortune doesn't just turn, it is spun, making it impossible to say where it will stop. Through the spinning of the Wheel, opportunities arise for our continual transformation. Like the Wheel, we are ever changing.

The Wheel of Fortune represents a moment when the Wheel is about to be spun. Generally it falls in our favor, but it usually brings a surprise with it. Prepare for the unexpected. Here is a clue for riding the Wheel: the closer one stands to the center, the less one is affected by the spinning.

Justice

Keywords: justice, karma, cause and effect, equality, truth, responsibility, integrity, fairness, judgment, contract, legal action, lawsuit, trial

Reversed: injustice, imbalance, dishonesty, hypocrisy, complications, abuse of power, red tape, bad decision

Astrological: Libra

Element: air

Symbols:

woman: virtue

between two pillars: the way of balance

upright sword: truth, justice

sword in right hand: active hand dispenses justice

scales: seeking fairness

scales in left hand: passive hand receives and weighs information

purple drape: sovereignty, spirituality, a higher justice

Justice is a time of karmic accounting. Justice will use her scales to dispassionately weigh all the relevant facts. Because she is not blindfolded like so many symbols of Justice, she does not reckon according to a single set of laws. She sees everything and carefully measures out the results. Using her sword, she applies both truth and justice to the situation. Unlike worldly justice, her determination is always fair.

XI · JUSTICE

Justice represents that it is time to reap what you've sown, for good or ill. There is no personal malice in this from the universe or anyone else, for it is nothing that you did not choose for yourself. Your response to this moment will become the next seeds that you sow. Make sure you plant only what you want to harvest.

XII · THE HANGED MAN

The Hanged Man

Keywords: reversal, letting go, sacrifice, suspension,
  surrender, withdrawal, restriction, crisis,
  delay, restraint, detachment, enlightenment,
  transformation, initiation

Reversed: limbo, martyrdom, indecision, self-sabotage,
  narrow-minded, punishment, imprisonment, treason

Astrological: Neptune

Element: water

Symbols:

  the tree/cross: deep spiritual beliefs rooted in tradition

  hanging upside down: letting go, seeing things
    from a different point of view

  calm face: accepting the situation

  halo: illumination, revelation

The Hanged Man willingly hangs from one foot. Why? Perhaps to see things from a different point of view. Perhaps it is some personal spiritual rite. Perhaps to see what would happen if he did. The tree from which he hangs is strong and deeply rooted, like his belief system. Instead of fighting against what must feel like an unnatural position, he relaxes and gives himself over to the experience. He sacrifices comfort and control, risks injury, and is rewarded with a revelation, a moment of enlightenment.

The Hanged Man represents a time of sacrifice. Approach it gracefully, even gratefully, because the experience will lead to deeper understanding. And by looking at things in a completely new way, you'll find answers that were hidden before.

THE MAJOR ARCANA

XIII · DEATH

Death

Keywords: death, rebirth, endings, mortality,
loss, change, failure, destruction, severing ties,
transitions, transformation, inexorable force,
elimination

Reversed: loss of hope, decay, corruption, depression,
inertia, holding on

Astrological: Scorpio

Element: water

Symbols:

skeletal figure: transience of life

white rose: purity and power

sunset: ending

While the Death card can mean physical death, it rarely
does. Instead, it is symbolic of the endings and transitions,
big and small, that are part of all lives. Whether the change
is expected or sudden, it cannot be avoided or denied. It will
happen whether we want it to or not. The characters in the
image show different reactions to death. The king resists
change, the bishop is prepared by tradition and faith, the
young woman knows just enough to be afraid, and the child
faces death with an innocent freedom from fear.

The Death card represents the ending of something and all
that experience entails, such as grief and mourning. As the
sun sets, it is just as easy to imagine it as a sunrise, promising
a new day. Every ending leads to a new beginning.

XIV • Temperance

Temperance

Keywords: temperance, self-control, balance, moderation, harmony, synthesis, patience, health, combination, blending, management, unification, synthesis, synergy, guides, angels

Reversed: imbalance, excess, temper, one-sided relationship, irreconcilable differences, short-term focus

Astrological: Sagittarius

Element: fire

Symbols:

angel: Archangel Michael, he who is like God

red wings: power

circle and dot headpiece: the sun, consciousness

triangle on garment: fire element

foot in water: emotions, subconscious

foot on land: material world, conscious

pouring water: tempering

Temperance means self-control, usually through moderation and a balanced approach to life. This is not as simple as it seems, for it is not merely about pouring out equal measures of everything. The alchemy of life is subtler and requires one to pay attention to circumstances, environment, self, and desired goals. For example, the idea of a balanced life usually means making room in daily life for work, rest, and play. However, there are times when such a moderate balance is not the best approach. Training for a marathon, studying for an exam, or planning a party or large event, for example, may call for more concentrated focus, for more time and attention.

Temperance represents the need to be very aware of your life, yourself, and your aims. With all of that in your consciousness, you can determine the perfect balance needed to achieve your desired outcome. This card is about the right parts coming together in a magical way to create something wonderful. Like alchemy, it is the transmutation of lead into gold.

The Devil

Keywords: bondage, obsession, materialism, temptation, shadow, fear, doubt, lies, violence, deviancy, ignorance, sexuality, hopelessness, lack of options, trapped, scapegoat

Reversed: abuse, addiction, violence, evil, weakness, detachment, breaking free, reclaiming power

Astrological: Capricorn

Element: earth

Symbols:

horned, winged creature: parody of Raphael in the Lovers

box: stability, tradition

man and woman: parody of man and woman in the Lovers

tails: mocking what it means to be human

loose chains: voluntary enslavement

hand gesture: parody of blessing in the Hierophant

torch pointing down: parody of the Magician

upside-down pentagram: material world valued over the spiritual

The Devil is a parody of the Magician, the Hierophant, and the Lovers. Knowing this helps explain this card. Parodies are usually clever and therefore attractive, just like the Devil. The Magician is about taking responsibility for one's life. The Hierophant and the Lovers represent walking according to our beliefs. The Devil, then, represents living in a way that is

XV · THE DEVIL

contrary to our beliefs and giving up control of our lives. It is often interpreted as bondage or addiction. The idea of being bound or controlled is apt, as the Devil (however it manifests) holds us back; we make no forward progress on our path, either spiritual or mundane.

The Devil represents a behavior or situation that holds us in bondage. It is usually not something forced upon us but rather is completely our own choice. Likewise, no one else will take the chains off us. We put them there; we must take them off.

XVI · The Tower

The Tower

Keywords: sudden change, upheaval, adversity, downfall, destruction, catastrophe, misery, disaster, ruin, chaos, release, awakening, freedom, escape

Reversed: fear of change, prolonged upheaval, obstacles, difficulties, losses, oppression, imprisonment, tyranny

Astrological: Mars

Element: fire

Symbols:

tower: belief system built up over time

lightning bolt: revelation that changes everything

stormy sky: confusion

The Tower took time to build and over the years became a very impressive edifice. In the same way, we create things such as homes, careers, relationships, or belief systems. Likewise, groups of people build things such as churches, organizations, governments, and businesses. All of these things become important parts of the structure of our lives. After a while, we cannot imagine our lives without them and cease questioning whether they remain true and useful. All of this is what the tower in this card represents.

The Tower card itself, though, represents that moment when we are forced to imagine life without the item because it, in short, no longer exists. A revelation has shaken the foundations and caused the edifice to crumble. In the aftermath, we see that parts were really no longer serving us. We pick up the pieces that remain true and strong and begin to rebuild, free to imagine a new way of life.

The Star

Keywords: hope, faith, healing, cleansing, renewal, guidance, peace, blessing, tranquility, serenity, inspiration, optimism, happiness, promises, wishes

Reversed: lack of faith, hopelessness, discouragement, feeling lost, broken dreams, dashed hopes, unfulfilled wishes, missed opportunities

Astrological: Aquarius

Element: air

Symbols:

nude woman: nothing hidden, vulnerability

ibis: the god Thoth

stars: eight minor astrological planets

larger star: clear guidance

foot on land: practical nature

foot on water: intuitive nature

pouring water: healing, cleansing, nourishing

pitchers: faith and trust

Stars play many roles, both mythic and mundane, in the lives of humans. We like to wish upon a star. Looking at the stars gives us perspective. Stars are used for navigation. The constellations tell stories. We use them to find understanding, direction, and hope. Their gentle yet brilliant light gives comforting hope in times of darkness. They are not illusionary like the moon nor overwhelming like the sun. They are soft, gentle, and yet amazingly powerful.

XVII • THE STAR

The Star represents refreshment and cleansing after trouble. It promises restored faith and renewed purpose when we are at our most vulnerable. As we pour our faith and trust into the world, we receive healing and guidance through the constant universal flow of the Divine.

XVIII · The Moon

The Moon

Keywords: secrets, illusion, deception, imagination, mystery, subconscious, confusion, falsehoods, cycles, bewilderment, anxiety, insecurity, dreams, nightmares, visions, psychic ability

Reversed: secrets revealed, mysteries unveiled, insomnia, trouble sleeping, irrationality, shadows, danger

Astrological: Pisces

Element: water

Symbols:

pool of water: subconscious

crayfish: deepest fears

domesticated dog: internal fears

wild dog: external fears

path: way through fear and confusion

towers: threshold

The Moon is a complex and uncertain card. Modern tarotists are hesitant to read it as strictly negative because of its association with feminine energy and the goddess. The moon appears to change in the sky each night, waxing and waning through its cycles, indicating a situation that is changing. What might be true today may not be true tomorrow. The moon reflects light, but it is shadowy and conceals as much as it reveals. Things that seem lovely in the moonlight may be monsters by the light of day, and vice versa. It heightens the gifts of intuition and creativity. It calls forth fears. It creates delusions.

The Moon says "be careful; things are not necessarily as they seem." This is a temporary state, so do not be distracted or tempted to veer from the path. Walking through the towers is crossing a threshold. After successfully facing fears, we will continue our journey with clarity.

The Sun

Keywords: happiness, joy, fun, optimism, enthusiasm, glory, clarity, consciousness, success, celebration, energy, vitality, good fortune, greatness, life

Reversed: ego, false impressions, delayed happiness, depression, burnt out, over exposure, drought, partial success, incomplete victory

Astrological: Sun

Element: fire

Symbols:

naked child and white horse: innocence, purity of will

red feather: will, desire, passion

red banner: desire for wholeness

sun: clarity, purity of thought, consciousness

walled garden behind: freedom

sunflowers: seeking gifts of the sun, optimism

Shining its brilliant warmth and vibrant energy, the Sun card brightens any reading. No matter what is going on, this card brings a positive attitude that can make anything possible. It is a fresh day and a new start. In the light of day everything is clear, and today all is right with the world. Optimism and enthusiasm reign, and everything we do seems gilded with success. We are filled with energy, and, like a new butterfly unfurling its wings to dry in the sun, we are eager to fly and embrace the adventure that is life.

XIX • THE SUN

The Sun represents a feeling or sense more than any specific event. It is the quintessential feeling of being present in a particularly fabulous moment regardless of circumstance.

XX · JUDGEMENT

Judgement

Keywords: rebirth, renewal, rite of passage, calling, vocation, awakening, change, decision, forgiveness, redemption, absolution, judgment

Reversed: doubt, forsaking vocation, ignoring a calling, avoiding change, unhealed wounds, lack of forgiveness, delay

Astrological: Pluto

Element: fire

Symbols:

angel: Gabriel, messenger of God

flag with red equal-armed cross: union of spirit and flesh

Gabriel sounds his horn. The dead hear the call and rise up, eager to embrace their new lives. Where is the "judgment" in this card? It is not people judging others but rather individuals judging their own lives and finding them wanting. After living in shades of gray and limbo, they are ready to add meaning and vibrancy back into their lives.

Judgement represents a calling that will lead to a life cleansed and full of possibilities. This card is also associated with forgiveness, but that is just a specific type of calling. If we are called upon to forgive and do, we are renewed and freed. If we do not and instead decide to foster a grudge, we remain as we are, trapped in anger or hurt. Anything that holds us in a lifeless, stagnant state can be the coffin from which we are summoned.

XXI · THE WORLD

The World

Keywords: completion, success, perfection, achievement, accomplishment, victory, reward, unity, wholeness, fulfillment, endings and beginnings, celebration, center of attention, travel

Reversed: delays, hesitations, false starts, stagnation, rut, incomplete work, lack of closure

Astrological: Saturn

Element: earth

Symbols:

laurel wreath: victory, achievement

two white wands: balanced, pure will

red ribbon lemniscate: eternal flow of passion

purple cloth: spirituality, nobility

the four fixed signs of the zodiac:

- Angel = Aquarius
- Eagle = Scorpio
- Lion = Lion
- Bull = Taurus

Hard work is crowned with glorious achievement. Attaining a goal brings pride, a sense of accomplishment, recognition, and rewards. The World marks the end of a journey. The laurel wreath of success creates a threshold through which we pass and embark on another journey, the beginning of our life after the achievement. Life is filled with endings and beginnings, some large, some small, some sad, some happy. This is one that is rather momentous and more than likely quite joyful.

The World represents the completion of a cycle in life or the achievement of an important goal and all requisite feelings and experiences that go with that. It is a time to enjoy what we've worked so hard for and to dream about possibilities for the future.

CHAPTER 3

THE MINOR ARCANA

The fifty-six cards of the Minor Arcana consist of two sets of cards, numbered and court, within four suits. The numbered cards run ace through ten and represent situations and events that make up daily life. The court cards include the page, knight, queen, and king; these represent the people in your life, including yourself.

The Minor Arcana's four suits—Wands, Cups, Swords, and Pentacles—each have their own full set of numbered and court cards. Each suit governs certain aspects of life:

Wands: will, passion, drive, career, projects, goals, desires

Cups: emotions, relationships, creativity, imagination, family and friends

Swords: intellect, thoughts, communication, truth, problems and solutions

Pentacles: physical world, resources and money, material life and work, health and the body

Minor Arcana Suit Correspondences

As mentioned earlier, tarot cards are often associated with other systems by way of correspondences. The four suits have more correspondences than any other aspect of tarot. The most common set of correspondences is elemental. This comparison is so ubiquitous that the elements are often used interchangeably with the suit names. Indeed, sometimes they are used instead of the traditional names.

Elemental Correspondences

Wands = Fire

Cups = Water

Swords = Air

Pentacles = Earth

- In some traditions, the associations for Wands and Swords are switched.

Comparing the elemental associations with the areas of life governed by each suit, it is easy to see how these became so closely related to the card meanings. The elements are tangible expressions of the suit meaning, making the energy of each suit easy to understand. Fire is an excellent expression of passion and drive. Water is often associated with the soul and creativity. Air blows away the cobwebs of illusion, revealing truth. Earth, being quite solid, is a literal representation of the physical world.

There are many other corresponding systems that are traditional. Traditional associations, mostly from the Golden Dawn, include alchemy, astrology, the Qabalah, and certain aspects of Christianity. Below is table of the most commonly used connections.

Traditional Correspondences

	WANDS	CUPS	SWORDS	PENTACLES
HEBREW LETTER	Yod	Heh	Vav	Heh
ALCHEMICAL STATE	Hot	Cold	Moist	Dry
ANGEL	Raphael	Gabriel	Michael	Uriel
GOSPEL	Mark	John	Matthew	Luke
ELEMENTAL BEING	Salamander	Undine	Sylph	Gnome
ANIMAL	Lion	Serpent/ Eagle	Man/Angel	Bull

Astrological Correspondences

Wands: Aries, Leo, and Sagittarius

Cups: Cancer, Scorpio, and Pisces

Swords: Gemini, Libra, and Aquarius

Pentacles: Taurus, Virgo, and Capricorn

Gender

The suits are often assigned gender, although this refers more to characteristics rather than actual physical gender. In general, "male" suits are considered active, proactive, and fast-moving, while the "female" suits are passive, receptive, and slower-moving.

Male Suits:

- Wands
- Swords

Female Suits:

- Cups
- Pentacles

The correspondences listed above are the most traditional and common ones used with the suits. However, they are by no means the only ones. The suits (and individual cards) have been associated with colors, seasons, directions, musical notes, scents, runes, and gemstones, to name a few. These correspondences do vary from practitioner to practitioner, so they are not included here.

Numbers and Tarot

Nearly everything in tarot is symbolic, and the numbers on the cards are no exception. Numerology (ascribing meaning to numbers) has a long history spread over many cultures such as Babylonian, Chinese, Hebrew, Christian, Egyptian, and, of course, Greek. Pythagoras, the sixth-century Greek mathematician, has had the most influence on modern numerology. That said, there is no absolute and complete set of numerical interpretations that is universally accepted.

Nevertheless, tarot readers often incorporate numerology into either their card interpretations or their reading style or even both. Below is a list of commonly used numeric meanings. You will see how these meanings manifest in the cards as you read about them. In chapter 5 you will learn ways to incorporate numbers into your reading apart from card interpretation.

1	individual, aggressor, self, leadership, yang, beginning of cycle, origin, seed, starting point, opportunity, gift
2	balance, union, receptive, partnership, yin, other, division, duality, debate, choices, psychic, intuition, empathic
3	communication/interaction, self-expression, innovative skills, result, output, productivity, abundance, creation, subconscious mind, imagination
4	order, construction, pragmatism, status quo, stability, equality, persistence, structure, stagnation, protection
5	action, restlessness, life experience, catalyst, instability, resistance, confrontation, difficulties, change, knowledge, teacher
6	home/family, responsibility, adjustment, collaboration, interaction, relationship, harmony, beauty, nurturing, healing, sympathy, comfort
7	thought/consciousness, spirit, observer, motive, imagination, inner work, psychology, contemplation, philosopher, sage
8	power, authority, achievement, abundance, execution of plans, action, movement, outer work, swiftness
9	highest level of changes, completion, end of cycle, fullness, readiness, ripeness, intensity
10	end, finality, depletion, exhaustion, excess

The Aces

All the aces are gifts or opportunities. They usually represent a short window of time. If you do not grasp the energy quickly, it will dissipate. Although they don't wait around long, aces are potent and intense. Aces also mark new beginnings and are considered a very positive sign.

· ACE OF WANDS ·

Ace of Wands

Keywords: desire, passion, will, drive, inspiration, potency, energy, enterprise, confidence, courage, optimism, setting goals, invention

Reversed: delay, dissatisfaction, lack of energy, impotence, a missed opportunity

Symbols:

hand of God: this is a gift or an opportunity

clouds: the opportunity will dissipate

landscape: dream big

wand: this gift is alive with potential

The Ace of Wands is like the universe giving you a big thumbs up. Whatever you are considering, just do it. Grab the opportunity and run with it. This is a gift with a lot of potential. If you feed and nurture it, you can create something really wonderful or at least have an exciting, inspired experience.

· ACE OF CUPS ·

Ace of Cups

Keywords: relationship, peace, love, healing, grace, creativity, joy, overwhelming emotions, intuition, affection

Reversed: separation, resentment, bitterness, stagnation, lack of connection, rejection of Spirit, a missed opportunity

Symbols:

hand of God: this is a gift or an opportunity

clouds: the opportunity will dissipate

dove and olive branch: grace, peace, and forgiveness

water: emotions, relationships, love

pink lotus blossoms: spiritual awakening, enlightenment, love

overflowing cup: this gift holds more than you can imagine

The Ace of Cups is like a chalice full of a magic potion with the ability to heal and renew the spirit. Let go of whatever emotions or judgments that are holding you back from what your heart wants, and drink deeply. It will nourish your soul and water the seeds of healthy, loving relationships or endeavors.

· ACE OF SWORDS ·

Ace of Swords

Keywords: logic, intellect, reason, truth, victory, decision, clarity, action plan, justice, knowledge, communication

Reversed: indecision, faulty logic, knee-jerk reaction, miscommunication, confusion, failure, injustice, a missed opportunity

Symbols:

hand of God: this is a gift or an opportunity

clouds: the opportunity will dissipate

crown with four points: the four elements (green = earth, blue = water, white = air, red = fire)

sword tip: the four elements are in service to Spirit

olive branch: peace

laurel branch: victory

the landscape: seeing the big picture

The Ace of Swords is a powerful weapon—a moment of truth that promises clarity, wise decisions, and sound plans. To use this gift to its best advantage, you have to see the big picture. If employed properly, you will clear mental clutter so you can move forward with confidence. Used impulsively or improperly, the sword can cause damage and pain. Wield it with love.

· ACE OF PENTACLES ·

Ace of Pentacles

Keywords: abundance, resources, money, wealth, health, comfort, pleasure, creation, luck, achieving goals

Reversed: lack, lost resources, physical concerns, seeking money for its own sake, a missed opportunity

Symbols:

hand of God: this is a gift or an opportunity

clouds: the opportunity will dissipate

pentacle: the elements of the physical world in service to spirit

gate: a threshold taking you from one world to another

white lilies: purity

Arthur Edward Waite wrote that the Ace of Pentacles is the "most favorable of all cards." It is the universe's way of saying this is your lucky day. Success is in the cards, and it is better than just money. This card promises worldly success and more. Your work will have ramifications in both the physical and spiritual realms. This ace holds the most potential of all the aces. Use it well!

The Twos

The twos capture moments of tension and balance. There is a sense of a decision needing to be made before the sequence of events can continue. The tension comes from knowing that the status quo in the image cannot be maintained forever and wanting to see what happens next.

· TWO OF WANDS ·

Two of Wands

Keywords: vision, energy, authority, ability, determination, dominance, intention, business or career proposal or decision, confidence

Reversed: indecision, confusion, lack of vision, a business deal falls through

Symbols:

precipice: operating from a strong position

globe: opportunity, resources, dominion

wand attached to building: safer choice or opportunity

wand in hand: riskier choice or opportunity

symbols on flag: the alchemical process from coarse material (black) to liquefaction (white) to ethereal (red)

The Two of Wands shows a situation fraught with decisions and opportunities. So many choices—and they all look promising! Most people would love to be in this situation, but studies show that more choices increase the possibility of paralysis, making it harder to make a decision. Wands are the element of fire, which tells us that will, passion, and courage should be employed rather than logic or emotions.

· TWO OF CUPS ·

Two of Cups

Keywords: union, partnership, connection, falling in love at first sight, harmony, love, feeling in love, kindred spirit, attraction, romance

Reversed: discord, argument, unrequited love, repulsion, rejection, rose-colored glasses

Symbols:

caduceus: communication

winged lion's head: elevation of animal desires

woman in blue: feminine energy

man in red: masculine energy

cups and hands touching: connection

cups at heart level: a heartfelt connection

rose-colored clouds: everything colored by romantic feelings

The moment described in this card is that feeling two people get when their eyes meet and they just know that something is there. It can apply to romantic interests, of course, but also to other types of relationships: business, platonic, even between a person and project, hobby, career, company, or organization. Whether the initial attraction will lead to a long-term relationship remains to be seen.

· TWO OF SWORDS ·

Two of Swords

Keywords: needing to make a decision, insufficient data, lack of facts, denial, feeling conflicted, head and heart in opposition

Reversed: ignoring facts, refusing to choose, lying to yourself

Symbols:

arms crossed over heart: not listening to the heart

blindfold: reliance on logic but not seeing all the facts

water: emotional wisdom

moon: intuitive wisdom

swords: desire to see all sides of a situation

The Two of Swords is the uncomfortable situation where the heart and the head want different things. Because you are lacking all the facts or the whole picture, you need to rely on either logic based on what is known or intuition. Because this is a sword, logic is probably preferred, as well as a strong desire to know more before deciding. However, some facts are not known, so our head may have to accept that this time the heart gets to choose.

• TWO OF PENTACLES •

Two of Pentacles

Keywords: multitasking, balance, tight budget, comparison shopping, allocating resources, calm or Zen-like behavior in face of crisis

Reversed: robbing Peter to pay Paul, financial distress, awkward situation, stress, frenetic energy

Symbols:

pentacles in lemniscate: maintaining balance in the physical world

ships at sea: going with the flow toward a destination

standing on balanced rocks: maintaining a challenging position

striped clothing: playfulness

large hat: ego

The Two of Pentacles indicates a time of necessary multitasking or budget balancing. Maintaining this activity can appear graceful to others, but it is challenging and can be stressful. The situation is temporary, and you only need to hold your balance for a short while. That is, only until either you decide what's got to give or something falls through the cracks. Then you'll be able to move forward instead of simply maintaining an impossible status quo.

The Threes

The number three is an important number to humans. It is, for some reason, inherently satisfying. Jokes usually include three steps before the punchline. Stories have beginnings, middles, and ends. We have the Triple Goddess (for Pagans) and the Holy Trinity (for Christians). Threes represent a level of completion, a logical conclusion, and a closed circuit.

· THREE OF WANDS ·

Three of Wands

Keywords: optimism, expectation, attraction, Law of Attraction, prepared, culmination, return on investment, focus

Reversed: delay, discouragement, missed opportunity, poor judgment, bad decision, distraction, dissatisfaction

Symbols:

high ground: able to see the big picture

ships: intentions and actions put into motion

symbols on cloak: focus, will, intention

large flowering wand: one main focus

clear skies: he can see his way clearly

flag on ship matching flower on wand: his intention is manifesting

The Three of Wands wraps up the ace and two very nicely. Beginning with an inspired idea followed by making good choices and taking action yields results. This card shows the positive fulfillment of expectations and decisions. While the ship isn't unloaded yet, it is in the harbor. Staying vigilant and focused leads to the successful culmination to endeavors and good return on investments. The cycle is nearly complete.

• THREE OF CUPS •

Three of Cups

Keywords: friendship, family, casual parties, joy, fun, abandon, abundance, celebration, connections, savoring the moment

Reversed: excessive partying, the morning after, awkward situations, feeling left out

Symbols:

lifted cups: celebrating and honoring friendship

woman in red: passion, emotions

woman in white: intellect, clarity

woman in green: earthiness, abundance

pumpkins: fruition, abundance

When people get together to enjoy each other's company, they are living the Three of Cups. Their diversity does not separate them, but rather their differences enhance their best qualities. The result is that everyone feels at their best. In addition, they are inclined to feel warm toward others. It is a complete cycle of warm affection and simple joy lacking in agendas or goals other than to celebrate the joy of life.

• THREE OF SWORDS •

Three of Swords

Keywords: unwelcome knowledge, painful truths, heartbreak, heartache, betrayal, disloyalty, unfaithfulness

Reversed: confusion, painful miscommunication, malicious words, hurtful lies, needless cruelty

Symbols:

swords: painful words or truths

heart: emotional reaction

barbed wire: emotions are trapped in pain

barren landscape: what was once alive is now dead

The Three of Swords shows how words can hurt and how the truth can cause pain. Truth and communication are the realm of Swords, but the destruction happens in the heart, slicing away what once was held dear. While feeling, honoring, and mourning the loss is necessary, it is all too easy to create a cycle of obsession where continued thinking keeps the pain fresh so that healing cannot occur.

· THREE OF PENTACLES ·

Three of Pentacles

Keywords: teamwork, creation, skilled work, making something of value, contributing to a worthwhile project, highlighting abilities

Reversed: ineffectual design by committee, shoddy work, not pulling your weight, not doing your best, contributions ignored

Symbols:

sculpture: physical expression of creative idea

in a church: working together for greater good

woman: intuition and creativity

man: rationality and planning

sculptor: physical skills

sculptor elevated: using skills for a higher goal

flower and cross: uniting abilities
to manifest inspiration

When inspiration meets excellent planning and is expressed through skilled hands, the result is usually excellent. When these three elements come together to achieve a higher purpose, the result is frequently phenomenal. The Three of Pentacles can represent achieving goals as a team or it can represent one person utilizing all three elements in his or her own creation. Whether collective or solitary, the cycle of inspiration to manifestation is complete.

The Fours

The number four, much like squares, is associated with stability, reliability, security, and, in extreme cases, stagnation. The number four acts as a container holding the essence, or energy, of each suit, creating a lack of movement. This can provide a needed rest in activity. However, not all the suits are shown to their best advantage while in a state of repose.

• FOUR OF WANDS •

Four of Wands

Keywords: holiday, party, celebration, gathering, honoring someone or something, successful completion of an endeavor, award ceremony, communal achievement

Reversed: plans go awry, celebrating too soon, discord, arguments

Symbols:

castle: event outside of normal daily life

wands and garland: a temporary structure for a celebration

fruit and flowers: abundance

welcoming girls: hospitality

The Four of Wands is a communal celebration that is more formal than the casual gathering of the Three of Cups. With the Four of Wands there is generally a reason for the party, such as getting a job, retiring, graduating, a birthday, family or class reunion, or a wedding. The fiery energy of the Wands plays beautifully in the container of the four as long as it is temporary. Enjoy the moment to the fullest, but when it is over, it's time to clean up and get back to work.

· FOUR OF CUPS ·

Four of Cups

Keywords: discontent, dissatisfaction, ennui, boredom, lack of gratitude, depression, resisting change, stagnation, lack of inspiration

Reversed: deeper depression, unhealthy or dangerous responses to boredom, taking pleasure in wallowing

Symbols:

tree: shelter, safety, tradition

cups on ground: unsatisfactory emotions or relationships

cup in hand: a fresh gift, something new

arms crossed over chest: heart is closed to new gifts

If water doesn't flow, it stagnates, and all sorts of slimy things start to grow. That may be great for a new ecosystem, but it's not a fitting state for the human soul. The Four of Cups represents being dissatisfied, for whatever reason, with what is present. Even though those cups are not wanted, the new one isn't either. The conflict is between maintaining the status quo, no matter how unfulfilling, or taking a chance on something new.

· FOUR OF SWORDS ·

Four of Swords

Keywords: rest, retreat, meditation, peace, recovery, regrouping, careful consideration

Reversed: denial, useless obsessing, procrastination, disordered thinking

Symbols:

three upright swords: challenges, concerns, problems, worries

horizontal sword: the mind at rest

angel with dove: peace and divine inspiration

When faced with a sticky problem, it is easy for the mind to wind itself up in endless loops of useless worry. This is not the case in this card, where thoughts take a well-needed break in the stability of the four. A calm retreat and quieting of the mind allows reception of what may appear to be divinely inspired answers. Lie down. Close your eyes. Breath in for four counts, hold it for four counts, exhale for four counts. Repeat until you feel relaxed. Finding the solution you seek will be easier than you thought.

• FOUR OF PENTACLES •

Four of Pentacles

Keywords: possessiveness, guarding and managing resources, saving, protecting, stewardship

Reversed: greediness, hoarding, taking what isn't yours, misuse of or carelessness with resources

Symbols:

throne on a block: stability and security

city in background: prosperity

man outside of city: outside the flow of material goods

pentacle above head: thoughts are on money or resources

pentacle in front of chest: money or resources are his dearest possessions

pentacles by feet: his life is built on money or resources

dull red cloak: stagnating passion

Pentacles are resources, which, in general, are meant to be used. If they are not, they fester, like fruit left to rot on the kitchen counter. There is, of course, a time for saving and withholding. The Four of Pentacles is one of those times. It is a tricky situation, though, because holding tightly to what you have can easily turn to stinginess or hoarding. Refusing to use resources also separates you from your larger community, potentially harming it and you in the process.

The Fives

The number five is chaotic and seems to exist to upset the stability of the number four. While adding energy to a stagnant situation might be necessary, it is a mixed bag, almost always bringing a crisis with it. The fives get a bad rap because they are often unpleasant, but they are part of the continuum of life. The tarot would be an incomplete tool without them. By understanding these troublesome cards, you can usually find a way to channel the energy of a situation toward a more desirable end.

• FIVE OF WANDS •

Five of Wands

Keywords: competition, conflict, debate, group efforts, committees, strong personalities, differing opinions, no shared goal, lack of leadership

Reversed: fights, aggressiveness, willfully causing trouble, unproductive criticism

Symbols:

different wands: individual wills or agendas

all on same level: equals or lack of a leader/authority

A group working together can achieve great things, as we've seen in the Three of Pentacles. However, in the Five of Wands, there is no agreement on what to do or how to do it. Everyone has an opinion. Brainstorming can be an excellent tool leading to the best possible ideas. Competition can bring out the best in people. Such volatile energy can quickly get out of control and lead to less productive clashes.

· FIVE OF CUPS ·

Five of Cups

Keywords: mourning, feelings of loss, sadness, regret, repentance, bitterness, frustration

Reversed: self-pity, obsessing over the past, beating yourself up, failure to mourn

Symbols:

three tipped cups: something that has been lost

two upright cups: what is left to take into the future

river: troubled emotions

castle: return to daily life

cloak and hood: being overwhelmed

cloudy sky: confusion and sadness

bridge: moving from old life to new life

The Five of Cups does not represent an actual loss so much as it represents the emotional reaction to a loss. Mourning is a natural part of life and essential to the healing process. Other parts of the process include taking stock of what is left and returning to normal life and adjusting. First, however, there is the grief, which can be overwhelming but should not be either avoided or wallowed in.

· FIVE OF SWORDS ·

Five of Swords

Keywords: victory, defeat, humiliation, aggression, poor sportsmanship

Reversed: a Pyrrhic victory, dishonor

Symbols:

swords: the prize, the spoils of war

man with swords: the apparent victor

men on the beach: the apparent losers

ocean: unfathomable situation

stormy skies: confusing situation, no clear truth, an ill omen

How are "victory" and "defeat" both keywords for this card? Swords are truth, and sometimes truth isn't always black and white. Such is the case here. There seems to be a victor, but at what cost? He seems to have made enemies, an action he may come to rue. The Five of Swords indicates that the whole situation is cloudy, and what might seem like the right action may not be. Try to see the whole picture and future consequences before going in for the "win."

• FIVE OF PENTACLES •

Five of Pentacles

Keywords: poverty, lack, need, hunger, bankruptcy, ruin, destitution, health concerns, rejecting help, being blind to possible aid

Reversed: neglecting yourself or your finances, relying on charity unnecessarily, taking advantage of others

Symbols:

crutch: relying on help, unable to stand on own

stained glass window: connection between physical and spiritual worlds

church: social, religious, and political aid

winter: the harshest time

The Five of Pentacles tells a sad tale of loss and destitution. The people in the card are in physical need: food, shelter, and health care. While there seems to be options available, they either are not interested or have been rejected. They are not totally alone. In this bleak picture of dire need, there is kindness and generosity between them. Although no one wants to get this card, we've all been there. Take steps to change the situation. Help is closer than you think.

The Sixes

The cards numbered five upset the stability established in the fours. In the aftermath of chaos, the sixes reestablish normality and calm. Roles are redefined, goals assessed, and rewards given. In creating the new normal, the sixes focus on collaboration and relationships. There are those helping and supporting and those receiving help and support. Part of interpreting these cards includes identifying which role you play in the situation.

• SIX OF WANDS •

Six of Wands

Keywords: victory, honor, achievement, recognition, pride, public ceremony, accolades, accomplishment, success, triumph

Reversed: failure, being overlooked, disappointment, humiliation, dishonor, shame, taking credit for someone else's work

Symbols:

laurel crown: victory, personal achievement

laurel wreath on staff: in memoriam
for the support of others

riding a horse: a hero

parade: public recognition and communal celebration

wands held by hero and others: a victory shared
by or benefiting the community

Here we have a triumphant parade, with the community gathered to hail the conquering hero. The Six of Wands promises recognition for success. While the achievement is personal, this card reminds us that nothing is achieved alone and that all heroes are supported in various ways by various people and communities. Consequently, the victory of the one is shared, in some degree, by all.

∾

· SIX OF CUPS ·

Six of Cups

Keywords: nostalgia, happy memories, kindness, innocence, selflessness, generosity, innocent pleasures, unconditional affection

Reversed: living in or romanticizing the past, insincere actions, manipulation, buying affection or friendship

Symbols:

flowers: gifts or kind actions

white flowers: purity, innocence

bigger child: the giver

smaller child: the receiver

guard and garden wall: protected area, separate from the outside world

house: protection and stability

The Six of Cups represents small, quiet, and often spontaneous moments of sweetness, rather like random acts of kindness. These moments come from the heart and, like a pebble thrown into a still pond, have far-reaching ramifications. This card can represent such a moment in the present or future. It also may be a memory of such an event that still warms the heart and affects behavior in a positive way.

· SIX OF SWORDS ·

Six of Swords

Keywords: journey, heading toward safety, escape,
flight, travel, assistance, admitting defeat,
impossible situation, protection, shelter

Reversed: remaining stuck, delay, worsening situation,
unseen danger

Symbols:

boat and oarsman: help or support

rough and calm water: moving from trouble to safety

swords in boat: some problems cannot be left behind

cloak/night: stealth and secrecy

Some situations are irreparable, and some relationships are irreconcilable. Even after the decision is made to leave such situations, help may be needed. The Six of Swords indicates just such a scenario, including the presence of the assistance required to safely exit a dangerous or unhealthy state. While this is a positive and perhaps necessary move, it will not solve everything. The scars incurred and truths learned will have to be dealt with once a safe harbor is reached.

THE MINOR ARCANA

· SIX OF PENTACLES ·

Six of Pentacles

Keywords: charity, fairness, gift, donation, grant, scholarship, loan, sound judgment, taxes, fees, sharing the wealth, asking for help

Reversed: denial of a grant or loan, stinginess, cheapness, uncharitable judgment, unfair taxes or fees, refusing to ask for or accept assistance, being unable to help when asked

Symbols:

prosperous businessman: authority combined with available resources

beggars: people in need of resources

scales: judgment or process involved in order to receive resources

Wealth is redistributed in a number ways. The Six of Pentacles includes most of those methods (such as charity, loans, grants, etc.) except earned income. If resources are needed, they are available for those willing go through the necessary processes. The card does not indicate that the request will be granted automatically. Someone with authority or ownership will make the final decision.

The Sevens

Life never stands still for long. Even though the return to balance in the sixes was welcome after the chaos of the fives, people are rarely content to remain in one place for long. As we reach certain levels of achievement, it is natural to assess our lives in order to determine our next steps. The sevens bring the energy of assessment into the forefront.

• SEVEN OF WANDS •

Seven of Wands

Keywords: defending, protecting, valor, courage, standing up for beliefs, bravery, resolve, taking action

Reversed: defensiveness, overreacting, being easily offended, looking for a fight

Symbols:

high ground: something worth defending

holding one wand against others: has made a choice

two different shoes: immediate action needed, no time for details

Taking a defensive position usually means that there is something worth fighting for. The Seven of Wands suggests that something needs protecting. It is time to stand up and face all comers. The fiery energy of the Wands usually indicates that events are moving quickly, so there isn't time to think or overthink. This is a case of knowing what is right and moving to defend whatever or whoever is in need.

· SEVEN OF CUPS ·

Seven of Cups

Keywords: confusion, fantasies, choices, imagination, dreams, illusions, lack of focus, wishful thinking

Reversed: fears, daydreams interfering with responsibilities, escapism

Symbols:

figure in shadow: will overshadowed by number of choices

snake: renewal or manipulation

dragon: bravery, battle

laurel wreath: victory, fame

jewels: riches

face: romance

tower: security

shrouded figure in cup: otherworldly pursuits

Options, possibilities, and choices! Tarot teaches the beauty of balance and shows us the effects of experiencing extremes. Having no choice or too many choices can be equally frustrating. The Seven of Cups indicates a time of many possibilities, some more realistic than others. Dreams have a lot of power and, if selected carefully, can turn into goals. Feeling confused or overwhelmed, however, can lead to inaction.

· SEVEN OF SWORDS ·

Seven of Swords

Keywords: stealing, rescuing, stealth, dishonesty, sabotage, sneakiness, stealth, traitor, spy

Reversed: exposure, failure of dishonorable plan, caught in the act

Symbols:

tents in distance: leaving community behind

red hat and boots: being driven by passion

The Seven of Swords is, at its most basic, about taking something away from someone or somewhere. Whether this is an act of theft or of rescue is unclear in the card and actually probably depends on the point of view of the individuals involved. When this card comes up, ask who is taking what from whom and why. Then, because the card has a prevailing sense of sneakiness, see if there is a more straightforward way of resolving the situation.

· SEVEN OF PENTACLES ·

Seven of Pentacles

Keywords: assessment, evaluation, reflection, measuring return on investment, harvest, rewards, appraisal

Reversed: disappointment, missed opportunity, harvesting too soon, plan didn't work out

Symbols:

vines: ongoing work

pentacles: results of work

After putting a lot of planning and work into a project, there comes a time to review the experience. Do the results measure up to the expectations? What worked? What didn't? What can be done in the future to improve the process? This applies to tangible projects, of course, but also to intangible aspects of life. Do actions taken within a relationship, for example, yield the desired outcome?

The Eights

The number eight is filled with power. This power usually propels one forward, often with great speed. However, if turned on its side, it becomes the infinity symbol. When this power becomes caught in an infinite loop, it turns into a trap.

· Eight of Wands ·

Eight of Wands

Keywords: speed, swiftness, events set in motion, travel, messages, communication, things running smoothly, reasonable consequences

Reversed: chaos, confusion, delays, frustration, swimming against the current

Symbols:

Aligned wands: events moving smoothly

The Eight of Wands brings speed and power to a reading. Events have been set in motion and are moving toward their logical conclusion. The outcome of the situation will not be a surprise; it will be the reasonable and expected one. Attempting to change the projected outcome would cause chaos. Traditionally this card also indicates messages and communication, as well as travel.

· EIGHT OF CUPS ·

Eight of Cups

Keywords: quest, journey, search, discontent, dissatisfaction, unhappiness, mission

Reversed: settling, accepting second best, running away, making excuses

Symbols:

broken pattern: something is missing

constellation: being guided

cloak, staff, pouch: taking a journey

The Eight of Cups is a bittersweet card. It describes a situation that is, on the surface, pretty good—almost acceptable. The problem, though, is that something is wrong; an essential element is missing. Until that key piece is found, no peace will be had; the situation will never be fully satisfying. This card marks the challenging beginning of a necessary journey. Leaving known comforts for the uncertain isn't easy, but in this case, it cannot be avoided.

· EIGHT OF SWORDS ·

Eight of Swords

Keywords: feeling trapped, restricted, dangerous situation, limited options, helplessness, complex problems

Reversed: victim mentality, giving up, seeing problems where none exist

Symbols:

blindfold: unable to see clearly

ropes: unable to move

surrounded by water: emotions influencing logic

This card depicts a fairly hopeless-looking situation. Being bound, blindfolded, and surrounded by swords and water makes taking any action very difficult. While it is clear that this is not an easy situation, there is advice within the card. Since this is the suit of Swords, logic and reason should be able to help. The presence of water indicates that emotions are present; however, they are making the situation worse. Putting emotions to rest for now and assessing the options logically will bring a solution.

· EIGHT OF PENTACLES ·

Eight of Pentacles

Keywords: work, skill, craftsmanship, artisan,
   diligence, dedication, focus, drive, determination,
   steady progress, satisfying work, attention to detail

Reversed: shoddy workmanship, workaholic, boring
   job, tediousness

Symbols:

simple pentacle: first efforts

intricate pentacle: mastering skills

The Eight of Pentacles embodies the saying that practice makes perfect. It suggests an opportunity to improve and grow in one's art or craft. The focus is on attention to detail and technical perfection. While the goal is the best product possible, the work itself also provides satisfaction. Tediousness is not a problem because of the enjoyment found in the task itself and because of the firm commitment to improving one's skills. Another saying for this card is that anything worth doing is worth doing well.

The Nines

All of the cards bearing the number nine, including the Major Arcana card the Hermit, feature a solitary figure. Folded into the idea of completion is the sense of solitariness. These cards focus on an individual's experience. There is something crucial that is discovered in these moments that shape our identity and mold the person we will become as we work through the situation. The situation itself forces us to face something at its utmost saturation.

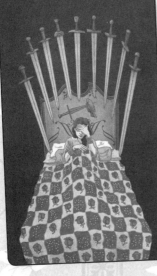

· NINE OF WANDS ·

Nine of Wands

Keywords: protecting, defending, stamina, loyalty, strength, discipline, wounded warrior

Reversed: hopeless cause, martyrdom, disloyalty, defensiveness, stubbornness

Symbols:

bandage: wounds

eight wands in background: something worth protecting

wand to lean on: ideal or belief that provides support

While similar to the Seven of Wands in some ways, the energy is very different in the Nine of Wands. In this card, the battle has been going on for some time and wounds have been suffered. The seven is the card of the battle; this card is the aftermath. The battle may be over, but it feels like the war isn't won. Although battered and bruised, there is still courage and strength remaining, and there is the sense that even if standing alone, there is no choice left but to continue to stand.

· NINE OF CUPS ·

Nine of Cups

Keywords: wishes fulfilled, contentment, satisfaction
with life, pride, hospitality, sensuality, worldly
pleasures, happiness

Reversed: overindulgence, smugness, dissatisfaction,
resting on laurels, selfishness

Symbols:

nine cups displayed: pride and contentment

cloths covering tables: something is hidden

Traditionally this is known as the "wish card." Fortunetell-
ers of old would ask a sitter to make a wish, and if this card
showed up in the reading, it meant the wish would come true.
In a reading it represents being content and satisfied with life.
The cloth covers the structure supporting the cups. An emotionally satisfying life takes work to create and maintain. Here
the focus is not on the effort but rather on the happiness.

· NINE OF SWORDS ·

Nine of Swords

Keywords: obsessive thoughts, sleeplessness, nightmares, worries, guilt, despair, oppression

Reversed: insomnia, overuse of sleeping aids

Symbols:

black background: bleak hours of the night

swords: thoughts and worries

red roses on quilt: passion

astrological symbols on quilt: order

slain dove: nightmares and worries that make peace impossible

The experience on the Nine of Swords is all too recognizable to most people. Who hasn't had the occasional sleeplessness fraught with obsessive thoughts? Instead of sleeping, time is spent worrying, replaying mistakes, or agonizing over a troubling situation. The logical mind, represented by the Swords, is fed from an emotional pool, leading to an ever-worsening nightmare. These cycles rarely yield anything useful but seem impossible to stop.

• NINE OF PENTACLES •

Nine of Pentacles

Keywords: discipline, self-confidence, individual achievement, material wealth, safety, security, solitude

Reversed: not following through, dissatisfaction, looking for external praise

Symbols:

lush garden: ripeness, riches, harvest

falcon: discipline

Venus symbol: love and values

snail: fertility, stability, security

The Nine of Pentacles represents that beautiful moment when a goal has been achieved and proves to be immensely satisfying. This card, though, indicates something more than a single goal. It is a sense of having built a life that suits one perfectly and is not dependent on anyone else. The whole situation is an homage to having confidence, knowing one's mind, acquiring the skills to achieve aims, and exerting the discipline to apply those skills.

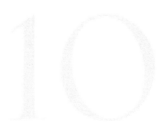

The Tens

The cards numbered ten all tell stories about completion, fulfillment, and excess. As the last of the numbered cards in each suit, they are literally the end of the line. Sometimes they are seen as the fulfillment of the promises made in the aces. Other times they embody the warning about having too much of a good thing.

· TEN OF WANDS ·

Ten of Wands

Keywords: burdens, obligations, numerous
   opportunities, duties, responsibilities

Reversed: physical exhaustion, oppression, tyranny,
   subjugation

Symbols:

   ten wands: projects and opportunities

   buds and leaves: all projects are being
      carried carefully and protected

Remember the opportunity promised in the Ace of Wands? It looks like more opportunities followed, and all of them looked too good to pass up—or perhaps some came with obligations or strings attached. The Ten of Wands is definitely too much of a good thing. While all the projects may be desirable or necessary, there are far too many of them. Some will have to be put down or all will be at risk of being damaged.

• TEN OF CUPS •

Ten of Cups

Keywords: family, domestic bliss, optimism, comfort, tranquility, peace, sanctuary, joy, happiness, deep affection

Reversed: family disputes, arguments, unhappiness, false front, separation, broken promises, betrayal

Symbols:

rainbow: promises or vows

stream: their affection flows through their lives

house: stability

A happy family, filled with dreams and hopes for the future, revel in their good fortune. The Ten of Cups symbolizes the best possible expression of the love between family members and very dear friends. Because this card is in the suit of Cups, it speaks more to the emotional ties and relationships between people rather than the physical home; that is found in the Ten of Pentacles. The sense of security that these relationships provide make it easy to feel safe and at home anywhere.

· TEN OF SWORDS ·

Ten of Swords

Keywords: surrender, ending, disaster, defeat, ruin, stop fighting, giving in, giving up, acknowledging ending

Reversed: melodrama, refusing to let go, denial

Symbols:

sky: sun rising or setting in background

red blanket: passion, blood

There is an old saying that "you can't win 'em all." The Ten of Swords is one of those situations that cannot be won. Despite a valiant effort—despite even, perhaps, "being right"—there is no victory to be found here. Continuing on will simply be a waste of energy. Just as the tens are the fulfillment of the aces, so the tens include the seed of a new ace. The light in the distance is both sunset and sunrise. The time for this fight is over. Get up, brush off, and start a new day.

• TEN OF PENTACLES •

Ten of Pentacles

Keywords: stable family, security, wealth, abun
comfort, roots, plans for the future, connectic
balanced and healthy life

Reversed: keeping up the Joneses, insincerity,
pretension, domestic troubles, debt, family problems

Symbols:

body language of child, woman, and
man: family connection

child: hopes and plans for the future

old man: connection between spiritual and
physical worlds, roots, traditions

white dogs: mundane life, loyalty, domestication

pentacles in Tree of Life pattern: daily
life infused with Spirit

The Ten of Pentacles promises not just abundance and comfort but the spirituality and enlightenment that make such a life meaningful. The family has roots, a legacy from past generations. An inheritance may be financial but it can also be traditions and values. The family has a future and so is inclined to guard and manage their resources. Together, they look on their past with pride and to the future with confidence.

CHAPTER 4

THE COURT CARDS

Traditionally the court cards have been considered the most challenging cards to learn. This may be because people try to study them as they would the other cards in the deck. However, by understanding the nature of the ranks first, it is much easier to learn to read these cards. So although you may be tempted to skip to the individual card meanings, these cards will make more sense if you consider the general principles discussed here first.

The court cards represent the people in our lives or aspects of ourselves. It is important to realize that gender in tarot is symbolic. Kings are portrayed as male to represent the active energy connected with the card. Queens are shown as female because the cards' energy is passive. Do not always assume that knights represent men and queens, women. The cards can sometimes represent events, particularly the pages, who can herald messages, or knights, who usher in fast-moving energy, although these meanings are more traditional and not used by modern readers as often as they used to be.

When learning the court cards, think of them as people and spend time getting to know their personalities. They all have characteristics that will help you understand the role they are likely to play in the situation being asked about and their unique motivations. Situations involving others can be unpredictable since we cannot control their decisions or actions. However, by understanding what drives them, you can find ways to work with them, eliminate friction, and focus on common goals or agree on mutually beneficial courses of action.

While each card represents a unique personality, there are shared commonalities based on rank and suit. So by understanding the characteristics of, for example, pages and the suit of Wands, you have a clear picture of the Page of Wands.

When considering the suit characteristics, the positive aspects generally apply to cards in the upright position, while negative qualities are usually read for cards that are reversed.

Wands

The fiery suit of Wands includes personality traits such as charisma, energy, optimism, charm, leadership, and warmth. The Wands court can be driven and passionate. They can also be self-centered, always wanting to be the center of attention. That warm personality may sometimes turn to anger in a flash, making them rash, immature, or cruel.

Cups

Members of the Cups royal family are often creative, empathetic, sympathetic, nurturing, sensitive, loving, intuitive, and caring. They are emotional and value relationships. They can also be needy, demanding a lot of attention from others in their lives, as well as overly sensitive and easily hurt.

Swords

Logic rules the Swords cards, and so we consider these folks able problem-solvers and plan-makers. They are often precise, witty, clever, intelligent, and excellent communicators. Sometimes they appear as cold-hearted and distant. Because they are so discerning, they are quick to pick up on weaknesses and can be known for their sharp tongues and cutting words.

Pentacles

Pentacles people are practical, loyal, and stable. They tend to value money, resources, and creature comforts. Luckily, they are also often good managers of such things. Because of their connection with the physical world, they can seem shallow. In addition, their precise accounting can lead to pettiness, and their stability can turn into dullness or stagnation.

Each suit has its own style and nature. All can fill certain roles, both positive and negative, and will do so in a way that reflects their suit. For example, all can be helpful in a crisis. Wands will take immediate action, Cups will provide emotional support, Swords will develop the best plan, and Pentacles will carry out the plan. All can be good friends in their own way. Wands will be your go-to for a good time,

Cups will be your shoulder to cry on, Swords will help rewrite your résumé or plan your vacation, Pentacles will go shopping with you or help with your budget. All can also be manipulative, with Wands egging you on, Cups playing on your guilt, Swords presenting a manipulative argument, and Pentacles offering temptation. All can be obsessive, with Wands worrying about their ego, Cups feeding their emotions until they block out all else, Swords arguing themselves into an ulcer, and Pentacles fretting about pennies.

As you gain understanding of the court card personalities and as you become more comfortable using your intuition in interpreting the cards, you will become more adept at identifying the people whom the court cards represent. Until then, or even after that, you may find it easier and even more useful to focus on the roles played by the card rather than just the individual represented. It is one thing to identify a person in a reading. It is another to know why the person is showing up, their goals, and how to best work with them. Understanding the roles represented by the rank will give you that information. Coupling that with the qualities they have based on suits will help you hone your understanding even further.

The roles played are determined largely by rank: page, knight, queen, or king. The rank also determines the extent of influence the person has on the situation. For example, the ramifications of the actions of a page will be very different from that of a king or even a knight. Rank also indicates how easily you can enlist the support of or change the actions of a person represented by that court card. You are likely to have an easier time talking a page into doing something than a

THE COURT CARDS

king. But by paying attention to the card's suit, you get a hint about their motivations and priorities so that you can figure out the best way to approach that particular person. Let's take a look at the ranks in terms of their basic meaning, sphere of influence, and accessibility.

Pages

Pages are young, either chronologically or in terms of the situation; that is, they may be inexperienced no matter their age. They are usually enthusiastic about learning or doing something new but also may be nervous because they are unsure of themselves. Pages don't have much authority or influence; rather, theirs is a supporting role. They are generally willing and eager to be included in projects. They are willing to help in order to be part of something larger. All the pages share curiosity, skepticism, courage, and fear. They all may feel slightly off-balance and grateful of support or guidance. In exchange, they can offer loyalty and enthusiasm.

Knights

Knights are among the most volatile of the court cards, often unpredictable, extreme, and chaotic. They are all about taking action. They can be single-minded and incredibly focused, always on whatever quest that has captured their attention. Knights are usually more interested in their own lives than that of anyone else. But they do have some power and ability, if not much experience or true authority. Whatever action they take will have an effect on the situation being read about, for good or ill. They are hard to control, especially when focused on their own pursuits. However, if you can capture their attention and convince them of your cause, they may well channel that intense energy toward your desired outcome.

Queens

More than any other court card, the queens seem most likely to actually want to help you. They have the disposition as well as the wisdom, experience, and power to do so. The queen's power is not always external or obvious. Like an iceberg, her influences are hidden, deep, and powerful. Although inclined to be helpful, queens are not pushovers. They are busy, involved people, which is one reason they are such great resources. They can also be tricky because they are so complex. Personal connection is important for them. If they take an instant liking to you, that's fabulous; just don't betray their trust. If they decide they don't care for you, it'll be hard to change that opinion. Solidify your connection or overcome a rift with common sense, such as recognizing her skills and experience. If she decides to connect with you, she can be a friend, a mentor, a cheerleader, or a role model.

Kings

In a reading, kings represent someone with authority who will affect the outcome of the situation. Kings make decisions, delegate, and have responsibility for individuals and groups. They usually have achieved some level of mastery, expertise, and accomplishment, and they are often concerned with maintaining the status quo. They may make final decisions about hiring, scholarships, loans, or insurance coverage, actions that could have a huge impact on someone's life. Because of their roles, kings are the least accessible of all the court cards. Gaining their attention isn't easy. When you do have it, you have to make the most of that opportunity. Sometimes that opportunity may not be in person but on paper, such as through a résumé or formal proposal or application.

Instead of memorizing lists of keywords and characteristics for court cards, it is most effective to use your basic understanding of their qualities (based on suit and rank) to interpret the card in terms of the reading you are doing. The interpretations below will focus on how to best engage or influence these cards based on their suit and rank.

Each group of court cards is set in a particular landscape that symbolizes their suit's characteristics. The Wands are located in the desert, as befits their fiery nature. The Cups are most comfortable by bodies of water, the tangible sign of their element. Swords prefer open, grassy plains where the sky is big and the air blows free. Pentacles nestle into lush, ripe landscapes, enjoying the fruits of their labor.

In addition to their suit's elemental association, each rank also has an elemental association. Kings are air, queens are water, knights are fire, and pages are earth. So we would say that the King of Swords is Air of Air, the King of Pentacles is Air of Earth, the Queen of Wands is Water of Fire, and so on.

· PAGE OF WANDS ·

Page of Wands

Symbols:

salamander: the element of fire

red jacket: being led by curiosity

wand held at distance: still examining, still learning

The Page of Wands is curious but lacks experience and confidence. Extend a guiding hand but be careful not to bruise his ego, as looking ridiculous and making a fool of himself (or having others make him a fool) is one of his fears. He doesn't like to sit still too long; inactivity makes him edgy and bored. He may need help curbing his need for external validation, anger, frustration, or temper tantrums. Give him the opportunity to explore, grow, and shine, and he'll be an energetic friend and supporter.

· PAGE OF CUPS ·

Page of Cups

Symbols:

lotus blossom: spiritual desire

fish: creativity, new idea, intuitive
message, possibly a secret

The Page of Cups fancies himself very deep, very true, and very serious. When he is involved in something that delights and fascinates him, he wants to dive in, revel in the experience, and learn all that he can. He opens himself up to it and is therefore very vulnerable. Guide him gently, helping him protect his heart without becoming cynical. Immaturity, unrealistic expectations, oversensitivity, and a tendency toward secretiveness may impede his growth. A more experienced hand can help navigate those waters and win a sweet and devoted friend.

· PAGE OF SWORDS ·

Page of Swords

Symbols:

wind: not knowing his own mind, tossed by the wind

large sword: reach exceeds grasp, needs experience

The Page of Swords is smart and tends to know it. He is a quick study, learning complicated ideas easily. He also has a deep love of and commitment to the truth for its own sake, often seeing situations in terms of black and white. He becomes frustrated when others cannot keep up and bored if not intellectually challenged. He's good with words and isn't shy about using them to get what he wants. If not actively engaged, he could fall prey to gossiping. Help him wield that razor-sharp mind to see the subtle shades of gray in the world.

· PAGE OF PENTACLES ·

Page of Pentacles

Symbols:

red headwrap: theoretical knowledge

hip bag: being prepared

floating pentacle: knowledge not fully integrated

The Page of Pentacles is interested in what he thinks of as "the real world." He wants to understand cause and effect and apply that knowledge to his own, albeit limited, resources. Being practical by nature, he values efficiency, but this trait can turn into laziness, just as his desire to acquire can turn to greediness. Give him a little to work with and let him see what he can do. He'll likely surprise you. A little guidance will be needed to help him see below the surface of the material and to understand that all ramifications and consequences aren't necessarily physical.

· KNIGHT OF WANDS ·

Knight of Wands

Symbols:

> *red feather:* driven by passion
>
> *salamander:* element of fire, some mastery
>
> *rearing horse:* high level of energy

The Knight of Wands is someone whose actions in this situation are fired by his will. He has something very specific he wants to achieve; he very much wants to have his way and will stop at nothing to get it. This knight is passionate about something and may heedlessly run roughshod over anyone in his way. If his will is in sync with the querent's, he will be a helpful influence. If not, the querent could get run over. Such intensity is often not maintained for very long, so it may be possible to just ride out this burst of energy.

• KNIGHT OF CUPS •

Knight of Cups

Symbols:

slow horse: moving slowly, dreamy and distracted

wings on helmet: association with Hermes,
messages from the Divine

fish: connection with water, emotions, and the soul

The Knight of Cups is someone whose current actions in this situation are motivated by emotion. His heart is focused on something—perhaps a vision, a quest, or a creation—or on someone. In this case, he is absolutely compelled to follow his heart to the exclusion of all else, for good or ill. At this point, he considers nothing else; all that matters is his presumed love, reconciliation, poetry, art, or dream. It will be very difficult to turn this knight's attention from his current pursuit.

• KNIGHT OF SWORDS •

Knight of Swords

Symbols:

> *fast horse:* thoughts racing through mind,
> acting quickly on thoughts
>
> *birds and butterflies:* connection with the
> element of air, thought, and logic

The Knight of Swords is someone whose actions in this situation are motivated by the commitment to an idea or a way of thinking. This person believes very strongly that his decision or belief system is the right one. He will use his skill with language and communication to do all he can to further his ideal. His weapons are logic, rational arguments, and evidence. He is prepared to use them to destroy any opposition. Because he moves so quickly, he will likely flail about dangerously, lacking in a larger plan or strategy. However, if you can catch his attention and get him focused on something, he will prove invaluable.

• Knight of Pentacles •

Knight of Pentacles

Symbols:

standing horse: slow moving, cautious

leaves on helmet and armor: governed
    by practical concerns

The Knight of Pentacles is someone whose actions are motivated by resources, finances, or the material world. Whatever he does is in order to further that goal. In this area timing can be everything, so he watches for just the right moment. He knows it's not just what you have and how you use it, but when you use it. He has the stamina and patience for the long haul. Although sometimes appearing passive or even weak, he is anything but. Alert and smart, he knows the value of active observing. When the time is right, he will make his move; he rarely takes a misstep. Of all the knights, he is the most reliable for a long-term project.

· QUEEN OF WANDS ·

Queen of Wands

Symbols:

> *sunflowers and lions:* association with
> the sun, fire, the sign of Leo
>
> *black cat:* intuition
>
> *legs open:* masculinity and assertiveness

The Queen of Wands is someone with a strong sense of self who wishes to inspire or help the querent. She understands the importance of personal power and strength of will. She can encourage the querent to boldness or force the querent into action. She is strong and confident and wants others to be, too, whether they are ready or not. The Queen of Wands is involved in this situation because doing so furthers her own agenda.

· QUEEN OF CUPS ·

Queen of Cups

Symbols:

mermaids and shells: association with
water, emotions, the soul

elaborate cup: values relationships and emotions

The Queen of Cups is someone who wishes to develop or nurture a relationship or to relate to, care for, or support a person on an emotional level in this situation. She is personally and emotionally involved or invested, generally in a healthy way. She feels, senses, or intuits the energies in the situation. Her guidance can be invaluable to the querent and is usually emotional, psychic, or creative in nature. This queen is generally supportive and helpful and can play the role of a patroness.

· QUEEN OF SWORDS ·

Queen of Swords

Symbols:

winged creatures: association with air,
logic, thoughts, and ideas

clouds on cloak: connection with water,
valuing relationships

The Queen of Swords is someone who can help or advise about an idea, problem, communication issue, or strategy. She is smart and experienced by having lived through both good times and bad. She will have ideas and advice about how to best achieve a goal. Consult her when working on a plan. She is particularly adept at exposing deceit and seeing the truth of a matter, and will express these plainly. She likely has her own agenda and can alter reality with a few well-chosen words. Double-check her suggestions against your own logic before jumping in.

• QUEEN OF PENTACLES •

Queen of Pentacles

Symbols:

goat: Capricorn, practicality, ambition

rabbit: prosperity and luck

dressed in red, white, and green: life, nature, and blood

simple garb in lush setting: natural world
more important than self

The Queen of Pentacles is someone who can get things done in an efficient manner with a beautiful or pleasing end result. In performing tasks, she is not as elaborate as the Queen of Cups, as elegant as the Queen of Swords, or as fast as the Queen of Wands, but all the details will be attended to and all resources will be used to their fullest potential. She can help the querent with any plans that require making the most of something or attention to detail. She has a knack for turning trash into treasure and making a bad situation as comfortable as possible.

· KING OF WANDS ·

King of Wands

Symbols:

    salamanders: the element of fire, total control

    lion: the sign of Leo

    flames on crown: passion

The King of Wands is fond of business, especially entrepreneurship. The King of Wands responds to passion and exciting ideas. To influence him or gain his support on a project, point out how the plan will further his own goals, engage his passion, or use his energy and resources in an exciting way. He does not respond as well to emotional pleas, excruciatingly reasoned arguments, or bottom lines. Spark his creative and energetic interest, and you will have his attention. However, his attention will be short-lived, so make the most of it.

· KING OF CUPS ·

King of Cups

Symbols:

> *floating on water:* experience navigating
>   relationships and emotions
>
> *fish:* soul, communication with the Divine

The King of Cups follows his heart and is moved by the hearts of others. Therefore, he can be found serving in areas such as counseling, health care, human services, the arts, and nonprofit organizations. Although sensitive and compassionate, he is not a pushover. He always feels his responsibility keenly. To enlist his support and influence his decisions, appeal to his sense of tolerance and the greater good. Childish, emotional outbursts will not have the desired effect. Temper pure emotion with wisdom and experience to gain his ear.

• KING OF SWORDS •

King of Swords

butterflies: association with air,
thought, ideas, and logic

lion's head with wings: elevation of animal desires

The King of Swords rules and is ruled by reason and logic. He delights in truth, enjoys communication, and finds comfort in clearly defined rules. He is driven by the conviction that he is doing what is right. Hence, we often find him involved in government, law, science, or medicine. When approaching the King of Swords, check all emotional pleas at the door. Don't expect excitement or passion to sway him. Focus on reason and logic, have all the points clearly defined, and express them as simply as possible. If you digress too much, you'll lose his attention.

· KING OF PENTACLES ·

King of Pentacles

Symbols:

> *rich clothes:* enjoyment of material world
>
> *lilies and roses:* purity and passion
>
> *bulls:* the sign of Taurus
>
> *castle in background:* abundance and security

The King of Pentacles is practical and values results. He likes things to run efficiently and effectively while producing something of quality. He tends to move in financial circles such as banking, investing, and real estate. Tangible goods also interest him, and he is an excellent salesperson. Because he values material goods, he might also work in protection or security. Finally, combining the desire for results and the physical world, coaching is a natural fit for him. Gaining his interest or support is easy: simply show him how an idea will make his life easier or more productive. Focus on both the bottom line and good quality, and you'll find him an attentive listener.

CHAPTER 5

READING THE CARDS

This final chapter shows you how to both become better acquainted with the cards and do a reading. It also gives you additional information about readings and provides practice techniques and a small collection of spreads.

Learning the Cards

There are seventy-eight cards in a tarot deck, so there is a lot to learn. Tarot is, by design, so well suited to the human experience—and, indeed, the human brain—that understanding and reading the cards is easy. These tips will make it even easier.

First, familiarize yourself with the structure of the deck, not just by reading about it but by laying out the cards in groups. Lay them out in groups, starting with the Major Arcana and then to the Minor Arcana's ace–ten, page, knight, queen, and king of each suit (Wands, Cups, Swords, and Pentacles).

Notice the progression as you move through the cards in a linear order. In the suits, notice how the energy progresses differently.

Then group them by numbers. Lay out the Magician, I, with the aces; the High Priestess, II, with the twos, and so on. Notice the commonalities as well as the differences.

As you explore your cards in these different ways, you probably will have noticed cards that have similar scenes or feelings. Group these together and explore their similarities and differences. For example, you might feel that the Lovers, the Two of Cups, the Ten of Cups, and the Ten of Pentacles share a similar energy, but notice their differences, too. Perhaps Death, the Tower, the Three of Swords, the Ten of Swords, and the Ten of Wands share a similar energy in your mind.

As you explore these connections, you might note them in a notebook or journal. In fact, that is another tried and true method of learning the cards. Keep a notebook so you can track these connections and record your thoughts on each card. Remember that while each card does have traditional meanings, your intuition is a valid source of knowledge. Add your responses to your notebook.

Experience is also a great teacher. Even if you feel like you don't know the book meanings, start doing readings right away without referring to the book. Keep track of your interpretations. You will be surprised how accurate you will be just based on your instinctive responses.

How to Do a Reading

Eventually you will develop your own reading style, adding special touches that reflect your beliefs and make the experience uniquely your own. Before that, you'll want to become comfortable with the basic structure of a reading.

1. Ask the Question

All readings answer a question, even if that question is *what do I need to know?* Before beginning the reading, it is essential to know what kind of information you are seeking. Be clear about your question. This may be a good time to think about your own personal ethics and belief system, as they will influence what kind of questions you ask. For example, some people will not read about someone who is not present or has not given their permission. Some will not read about health, legal, or financial issues. Some will not make predictions about the future. You need to define for yourself the ethical boundaries you will maintain. Working with tarot is a powerful experience, and as a reader you are responsible for the readings you give. So consider the importance of personal ethics very carefully before you agree to answer any question.

2. Pick a Spread

This book contains a few spreads that can cover many situations. Other spreads are readily available in other books and on the Internet. You can also create your spreads. If you are interested in expanding your collection and understanding of spreads, consult my book *Tarot Spreads: Layouts & Techniques to Empower Your Readings*. When considering a spread, think about the question and review the spreads beginning on page 238 to determine which spread can best answer it.

3. Shuffle Your Cards

You can shuffle any way you like as long as it effectively randomizes the cards. If you prefer not to shuffle, you can simply fan out the cards and randomly select the number needed for the spread you selected. If you are reading for someone else, you may wish to have them shuffle or select the cards.

4. Lay Out the Cards

Lay out the cards according the spread you've selected. Some readers lay the cards face down. They then turn the cards up one by one and interpret them as they go along. However, it is more effective to lay them face up in order to scan the reading for important preliminary information. We will discuss this practice next.

5. Interpret the Reading

This part is the longest, most involved part of the reading. Below is a systematic approach that gives clear, concise, and focused answers.

Begin by scanning all the cards in a reading. Scanning creates a framework, gives focus, and provides useful information about the situation being explored in the reading.

Scanning takes note of the numbers, suits, and other symbolic or otherwise abstract elements of a card separate from the image and the individual card interpretation. Scanning can help identify timing. It lets you know what aspects of a querent are affected or at play in a situation. A quick analysis of

READING THE CARDS

the suits can let you know if anything important is missing or if there is an energetic block.

This technique is presented as a series of steps. However, reading the cards is an art and things do not always happen in a linear fashion. Find your own rhythm and flow, and be open to the flow of each particular reading.

A. Look for Major Arcana Cards

These cards represent energy and events beyond the querent's control. If there are a disproportionate number of Majors in the reading, the querent has less control over events and is likely in the midst of learning an important life lesson.

B. Look for the Court Cards

If there are a disproportionate number of court cards, too many people are involved in the situation or the querent is having identity issues. If the reading (and situation) feels confused, start weeding out the influences of others and bring the focus back on the querent.

C. Analyze the Suits Present

Are the four suits equally represented? If not, what does that say about the situation? If many Swords are present, the querent may be in their head too much. Cups? Overly emotional. Seek to bring balance, if necessary. What does the absence of suit mean? What does the lack of Cups tell you about a relationship reading?

D. Check the Numbers

If there is more than one of any particular number in the spread, pay attention to those associations. For example:

- If there are multiple aces, there is a focus on new beginnings or fresh opportunities.
- If there are multiple twos, there is a focus on choices or relationships.
- If there are multiple threes, there is a focus on creativity or teamwork.
- If there are multiple fours, there is a focus on stability or stagnation.
- If there are multiple fives, there is a focus on conflict, loss, or chaos.
- If there are multiple sixes, there is a focus on communication, community, or problem solving.
- If there are multiple sevens, there is a focus on reflection or assessment.
- If there are multiple eights, there is a focus on movement, speed, or power.
- If there are multiple nines, there is a focus on independence or solitude.
- If there are multiple tens, there is a focus on something coming to an end.

You can use the numbers in a different way as well. Oftentimes in a reading, we want to see what a situation is like and how we might change the outcome. Knowing how far advanced a situation is lets us know how easily we might change the outcome. For example, if a relationship is in the early stages, consisting of just a few casual dates, it is very simple to end that relationship. The longer a relationship goes on, the more the lives of the couple become intertwined and the more energy it takes to end that relationship.

If there are a large number of aces, twos, or threes, the situation is in the early stages of development, so it is most easily influenced or changed.

If there are a large number of fours, fives, or sixes, the situation is in the middle phase and will require more effort to change.

If there are a large number of sevens, eights, or nines, the situation is well entrenched and will require considerable effort to change.

If there are a large number of tens, the situation is nearly resolved and may be very difficult (although not necessarily impossible) to change.

E. Look at the Visual Pattern Made By the Cards

Step back and look at your reading as one large picture. Look at the colors. What do they tell you about the situation? Look for repeated symbols and consider their significance.

F. Interpret Individual Cards

Once you've scanned the cards as a whole, interpret the individual cards, keeping in mind the question asked and the positional meaning as defined by the spread you selected.

How to Practice Readings

Learning the card meanings and reading techniques is one part of becoming a good card reader. Another essential element is practice. The more readings you do, the more confident you will become and the more comfortable you will be, which generally leads to better readings. There are a number ways to practice. Friends and family are often agreeable to being guinea pigs. This is a good way to practice, as it includes the all-important interpersonal interaction. There are two downsides to keep in mind. First, if you know your querent too well, you may fill in the blanks with what you know rather than reading the cards, and, second, objectivity may be an issue, and it may be too easy to give the advice you wish to give regardless of what the cards may actually say.

Doing readings for yourself is a good way to practice, too. However, it has its own set of downsides. Besides the whole issue of knowing yourself and lack of objectivity, there is the fact that you only have so many questions. Once you run out of questions, there is nothing wrong with doing readings for small, everyday questions and situations as long as you realize it is just for practice and you do not become dependent on readings to function in your life. Once you become a more experienced reader, there will probably be times you want to read for yourself in a serious way. Tips for reading successfully and effectively for yourself can be found later in the chapter.

One of the benefits of practice is feedback. The only way to get real feedback is to read for people with whom you can maintain contact, so that you can follow up. Reading about the lives of celebrities is another way to get feedback—well, a kind of feedback. Usually with celebrity news a story is reported, and if it is about an affair or an illness or movie negotiations there is usually a follow-up story, and that is how you get feedback. One thing to consider here is your own personal ethics. If you have determined that you will not read for someone without their permission, then you probably won't read for celebrities. Some readers do bend that rule, saying that the reading will only ever be seen by themselves, but you must decide for yourself what is right.

If you have a favorite weekly TV show, that is a great opportunity to practice readings. Each week before you watch the most recent episode, do a reading. Watch the show and get instant feedback. This also works for movies and books. The downside to this method is, again, one of ethics. Some people believe that a reading is a sacred conversation with the Divine and that reading for fictional characters is disrespectful. Others think that the Divine fully understands and supports their need to practice. As usual, this is for you to think about and ultimately decide.

Whatever method you decide, practice as much as you can. No amount of reading or studying can make up for lack of experience.

Significators

Significators are cards that are selected before a reading to represent the querent. Traditionally, significators were selected and then set aside as a focal point for the reading. This had the unfortunate result of taking a card out of play for no apparent reason. Because of this, many modern readers do not use significators. Other readers will select a significator card and include it in the reading.

The oldest traditions advised a reader to use the High Priestess for all female querents and the Magician for all male querents. This method is almost never used now, as the High

Priestess and the Magician are such important cards that it does not make sense to remove them from the deck.

More commonly, readers select the significator from the court cards. This makes sense because the court cards represent people. If you opt to use a significator, try including it in the reading. This can be useful, as you will learn how the querent responds to or feels about other cards. For example, the Page of Cups would probably be happier to find the Two of Cups in her reading than the Knight of Swords. The Page of Cups is interested in love and likely eager to experience a new relationship, while the Knight of Swords is more often than not too focused on something else and might think of a new relationship as someone in his way rather than a gift.

To select a significator from among the court cards, first determine which suit best represents the querent based on physical appearance, astrological sign, or personality. Then select the appropriate rank based on age. One of the weaknesses of the traditional physical appearance method is that every permutation of skin/hair/eye color is not represented.

Physical Appearance

Wands: fair skin with blond hair and blue eyes

Cups: light to medium skin with light brown hair and blue or hazel eyes

Swords: olive skin with dark hair and light eyes

Pentacles: dark skin with dark hair and dark eyes

Astrological Sign

Wands: Aries, Leo, and Sagittarius

Cups: Cancer, Scorpio, and Pisces

Swords: Gemini, Libra, and Aquarius

Pentacles: Taurus, Virgo, and Capricorn

Personality

Wands: a fiery, passionate, energetic person

Cups: an emotional, sensitive, creative person

Swords: an intellectual, logical person

Pentacles: a down-to-earth, practical person

Age

Page: a child or young woman

Knight: a young man

Queen: a woman

King: a mature man

Picking a significator in this way has the benefit and mystique of tradition. However, tarot readers throughout time have always been an experimental bunch. Some prefer to let the deck pick the significator by shuffling the whole deck and using the card on top as the significator. Others ask the querent to look through either the whole deck or just the court cards and select one that they think represents themselves in the situation, asking them why they made that choice. This allows the querent to touch the cards, which involves them in the reading, and it allows the reader to learn how the querent views themselves in the situation.

How to Read for Yourself

One of the reasons readings for ourselves can be unsatisfying is that we don't treat readings for ourselves with the same respect as we do when we read for others. When reading for someone else, most readers prepare themselves in some way, whether it is a ritual, meditation, saying a quick blessing, lighting a candle, etc. We should take just as long—and, in some ways, longer—to prepare for reading for ourselves. The points below will help you prepare for a self-reading, clarify your question, and interpret the reading with objectivity.

1. Calm, Center, and Ground

Like any other person, when we are in the throes of emotional turmoil, we want instant answers and comfort. Most readers agree that it is not optimal to read for someone in a highly charged state. So whatever the level of your emotional state, make sure you are calm and can approach the cards with as much objectivity as possible. This may take just a short meditation or a few deep breaths, or it may take a day or two. Giving your emotions space and honoring them is necessary if you are to tap into your logical and intuitive skills with clarity.

There are many ways to center and ground. If you already have a method that works for you, use that. If not, try this simple technique. Sit with your arms and legs uncrossed and your feet flat on the floor. Close your eyes and breathe in for four counts, hold for four, exhale for four, and hold again for four. Repeat this three times or as many times as needed to calm your heart rate and relax. Imagine a white light for whatever you consider the source of the Divine coming into the crown of your head. Imagine roots extending from your feet deep into the earth. Breathe in one long, slow, deep breath. Exhale and imagine all that is unnecessary, all that is distracting, releasing down into the earth. Inhale again, long and slow, and imagine the light entering you, filling in all the space that is now empty of all that is unneeded at this time.

2. Write Out Your Question

There is something about writing that forces us to be precise. Also, the act of reflecting upon your question will help you see the layers and perhaps unnoticed aspects of the question. Imagine that someone else came to you with this question. What, if anything, would you ask them before proceeding? Do the same for yourself.

3. Think About the Answer You Hope For

One of the pitfalls of reading for yourself is spinning whatever cards come up to suit what you hope will be the answer. Once you've thought about what you would consider your "best-case scenario" answer, think about the cards that might come up to represent that answer. Write them down and why you think they'd herald that answer.

4. Think About the Answer You Dread

What would be the answer you *don't* want to see? Think about the cards that would represent that scenario. Write them down and include why they would indicate that outcome. This is important. No one wants bad news, so it is easy to justify any spin we put on the cards that might come up.

By identifying ahead of time what these cards might be, it is easier to be honest with yourself.

You can do this for as many variations on possible outcomes as you like. You are not limited to only the "worst" and "best." The more signposts you create for yourself, the easier it will be to honestly interpret the cards.

5. Make Your Reading an Event

Treat it as you would a reading for a friend or client. If you light candles, set up a nice space, and ask for guidance from a deity, the universe, a guide, or your higher self, do this for yourself. Consulting your cards—employing your skills and gifts—has worth, so value them just as equally when you read for yourself.

6. One Reading Only

Just as many readers will only read for a specific question once in an allotted time period, determine that no matter what your reading says, you will only read once on this topic. A reading is an opportunity to converse with the Divine. Respect that by respecting the cards that are revealed, and do not scoop them up in a fit of pique and start over.

7. You Are Your Own Client

Imagine that you, in your role as the reader, are channeling your higher self, guide, or source of wisdom. As the reader, interpret the reading out loud, using your name as if you are talking to yourself, which you are. If possible, record the reading. Many readers, when they are in the flow or feeling tapped in, don't always remember what they say as they interpret the reading. If you record yourself, you will not miss any important messages.

8. Eschew Clarifiers

A clarifier is a card that many readers pull in addition to the cards dealt in the reading. It is meant to clarify a card that a reader finds problematic in the reading. Clarifiers are overused and often add to the perceived confusion rather than actually adding understanding. They can become a crutch to avoid a card that is not particularly liked or understood. Instead, try to stick with the cards that are present; they are there for a reason. If you are well and truly stuck, let the reading sit for a day or two and then come back to it with fresh eyes or meditate on the card that is causing the roadblock. Memorize the card, close your eyes, and step into the card. Ask any characters or creatures present the questions you have about the card. The ego has ways of protecting itself, so the card may contain wisdom that the ego is not willing to hear. Going into a meditative state may make it easier to quell the ego and find the treasure in what at first glance appears to be an unfathomable or troubling card.

9. End Strong

No matter what the outcome of the reading, include an action step. While there are some things truly beyond your control, no matter what happens, you always have the opportunity to take some kind of action or learn some kind of lesson. Leave yourself with the same optimism and sense of empowerment that you would give any friend or client.

10. A Technique

If you are reading about two or more choices, this technique is a great way to help with objectivity. Write your choices on separate small pieces of paper. Fold them and mix them up so you don't know which is which. Lay them on the table—do whatever you need to do to make sure you truly don't know which is which—then pull cards for each piece of paper and interpret the mini readings. Without looking at the papers, decide which one you want simply based on the cards pulled. Then look at the paper, and you'll have your answer.

11. Second Opinions

Have a group of readers you trust and can go to for readings. Many readers have readers, just as priests have confessors and therapists have therapists.

Reading for yourself can challenging, but—as with anything else—a little practice, patience, and intelligence will go a long way toward turning it into a very rewarding activity.

Spreads

Spreads are the framework for any reading. They provide shape and structure for the interpretation and an ultimate answer or advice to give to the querent. The choice of spread is just as important as the wording of the question. Carefully wording your question and selecting a spread that can answer the question will help make your reading as useful and complete as possible.

Spreads range in size from a single card to the full deck. The only way to know which ones work best for you is to try

as many as you can. Readers who like to delve dee
card will prefer smaller spreads. Those who like t
patterns within the cards will use larger spreads.

How many spreads does a reader need? That depends on the reader. Some readers find one spread, such as the Celtic Cross, that they can use for any question. Others have a small collection of spreads to suit many purposes. Still others love collecting and trying out new spreads. The few included here can get you started and are designed to answer most questions.

Spread design is an interesting part of tarot practice. If you are interested either in learning more spreads or creating your own, my book *Tarot Spreads: Layouts & Techniques to Empower Your Readings* should prove useful.

One-Card Spread

Sometimes less is more. There is a simple clarity to a one-card answer. Conversely, if it is true that a picture is worth a thousand words, then it is possible to find great depth and wisdom in just one card. And the beauty of this "spread" is that it can be used to answer almost any question. Simply ask the question and draw one card. For example:

- What do I need to know today?
- What should I do about _____?
- What is the perfect gift for my niece?
- What will I enjoy more, going to the party or staying home and relaxing?
- How can I _____?
- What is the root of this anxious feeling?

Three-Card Readings

Three-cards spreads are great starter spreads, as well as being great go-to spreads for more seasoned readers. Three cards are not overwhelming but do provide some material to work with. Part of a good reading—the part that is hard to teach in a book—is the interaction between the cards and how they affect each other's meanings. Working with three cards, you can practice noticing those influences in a manageable format. Here are some common three-card spreads:

- Past, Present, Future
- The Situation, The Problem, The Solution
- The Decision, Choice 1, Choice 2
- The Situation, What To Do, What Not To Do
- The Situation, Challenge, Advice

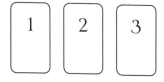

Celtic Cross Spread

The Celtic Cross spread is a very traditional and well-known spread that is included in almost every tarot book. There is a reason it is so well known and popular: it provides a wealth of information about any situation. There are enough cards to provide plenty of material to work with. It gives a clear overview of a situation as well as the probable outcome. It can be read as a large spread or as a series of smaller spreads.

Because the Celtic Cross spread has been around for over one hundred years (it was invented by Arthur E. Waite, who falsely claimed it was an ancient spread), there are many variations. You may see versions that label the positions slightly differently. Remember, tarot has and continues to evolve, and that goes for spreads, too. It's okay. Don't assume that one variation is wrong and the other is right. In addition to a variety of positional meanings, people have altered or added to the Celtic Cross layout. As you work with it, if you notice areas or types of information that you'd like, add positions and see how they work out.

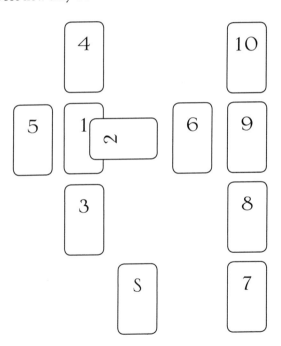

S. Significator

1. Covers: the influence that is affecting the querent or the situation

2. Crosses: the obstacles or energies working against the querent in this situation

3. Crown: the querent's ideal or goal in the situation

4. Foundation: the basis or foundation of the situation

5. Behind: influences that affected the querent or situation but are now passing away

6. Before: what is likely to happen next

7. Yourself: how the querent sees him- or herself in the situation

8. Your House: the influences of circumstances or people surrounding the querent

9. Hopes and Fears: the querent's hopes or fears regarding this situation

10. What Will Come: the culmination, resolution, or outcome of the situation

This spread was originally designed for purely predictive readings, and the position meanings show that. For this or any spread you try, always tweak the meanings so that they make sense with your beliefs and your reading style. For example, if you do not like how "the culmination, resolution, or outcome of the situation" implies a sense of absolute, written-in-stone fate, change it to something like "the current most likely outcome if all things remain as they are."

If the outcome isn't to the querent's liking, a common practice is to follow up with another short one- to three-card reading to advise the querent about how to change that outcome.

As mentioned earlier, the Celtic Cross can be read as several mini spreads as well as one large one. For example, the first mini spread is the cross in the center made up of the significator, the covering card, and the crossing card. Read together, these cards concisely create a picture of the situation or conflict concerning the querent. Card 5, the significator, and card 6 together make the familiar three-card spread of Past-Present-Future. Cards 6 and 10 show the trend of future events. Cards 3 and 9 tell what the querent wants, hopes for, or fears. Reading these cards in these combinations also allows you to use your skills in reading card pairs to add nuances to the reading.

Horseshoe Spread

The Horseshoe spread is another popular general-use spread.

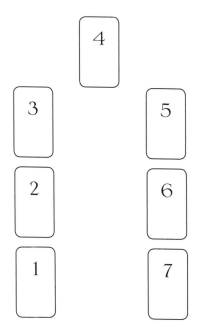

1. Past: energy from the past that affects the present situation

2. Present: the current state of the situation

3. Future: the potential future if nothing changes

4. Querent: how the querent sees him- or herself in the situation

5. Additional information: what can help the querent in this situation

6. Challenge: a problem to be overcome

7. Outcome: a possible future if the querent takes
   action

Variation: Try using a significator in position 4.

Making a Choice Spread

Having the luxury of choice is great, but sometimes it
is hard to decide what is the better option. This spread is
designed to help with that very situation. Cards 2, 3, and 4
represent choice A. Cards 5, 6, and 7 represent choice B.

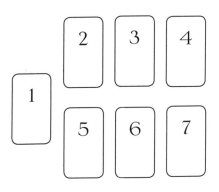

1. How you feel about the choices

2 and 5: The benefits of each choice

3 and 6: the downsides of each choice

4 and 7: the probable outcome of each choice

Variation: If you have more than two choices, simply
add rows to accommodate any other options. Also,
if you have specific items to compare, add columns.
For example, if you are looking at two job offers, you
could alter the spread as follows:

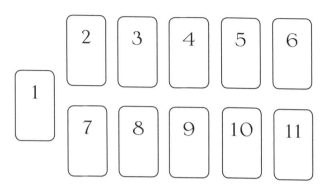

1. How you feel about the choices

2 and 7: salary

3 and 8: benefits

4 and 9: emotional satisfaction

5 and 10: company culture

6 and 11: ability to grow

CONCLUSION

Studying tarot is a layered and rewarding endeavor. Each individual card is a portal to worlds to explore, providing gateways to imagination and springboards for intuition. The many associations for the cards can lead to other areas to learn about, such as astrology and numerology. Eventually the cards will become seventy-eight trusted and wise friends that can help you navigate your life and lead you to spiritual growth. You will learn to better understand yourself and others. If you read for others, you can share these gifts with them, helping solve problems, create better lives, and heal wounds.

Tarot's long history is a rich field to plumb and includes the Renaissance, art, alchemy, nineteenth-century esoteric arts and secret societies, and spirituality. The future of tarot, an ever-evolving art and craft, is wide open. As you experiment and develop your own practices, you will add your mark to tarot's history.

The reading list that follows provides some suggestions as to what aspect of tarot you might delve into next. Armed now with your faithful deck of cards and a good foundation, go forth and explore! Play with your cards, seek wisdom, find and provide guidance, and, above all, continue to learn.

SUGGESTED READING

Sylvia Abraham, *How to Use Tarot Spreads*
Over three dozen tarot spreads; can be used with any tarot deck.

Ruth Ann and Wald Amberstone,
   The Secret Language of Tarot
A study of common symbols used in tarot cards. Theoretically it can be used with any deck but is based on RWS.

Nancy Antenucci and Melanie Howard,
   Psychic Tarot
This book teaches tarot readers how to use their intuition to read the cards and how to strengthen their psychic abilities.

Ly de Angeles, *Tarot Theory and Practice*
Includes basic card meanings and a very interesting method of conducting a reading. Meanings are based on RWS, but the reading can be conducted with any tarot deck.

Josephine Ellershaw, *Easy Tarot Reading*

A fantastic explanation of how a reader weaves tarot card meanings into a seamless, useful interpretation.

Mary K. Greer's 21 Ways to Read a Tarot Card

An excellent book for deepening your understanding of tarot cards; can be used with any deck.

Mary K. Greer, *The Complete Book of Tarot Reversals*

A guide to understanding and using reversals in tarot readings using decks in the RWS tradition.

Elizabeth Hazel, *Tarot Decoded*

If you are interested in learning about dignities and more about correspondences, this is an excellent resource. Can be used with any deck.

Kim Huggens, *Tarot 101*

A complete course in studying tarot cards to develop deeper meanings. Takes the unique approach of grouping cards by similarity of meaning rather than in numeric order; can be used with any deck.

Marcus Katz and Tali Goodwin,
   Around the Tarot in 78 Days

A comprehensive course covering one card per day. In-depth, solid material presented in a very accessible manner.

Corrine Kenner, *Tarot Journaling*

This book is out of print, but if you like journaling, find a used copy. It is filled with excellent journaling ideas and can be used with any deck.

Llewellyn, *Llewellyn's Tarot Reader*

An annual published from 2005 through 2008 filled with excellent articles, spreads, and deck reviews. Although all issues are out of print, used copies are on the market.

Barbara Moore, *Tarot for Beginners*

This book showcases how to read different decks by focusing on the images in relation to traditional RWS meanings.

Barbara Moore, *Tarot Spreads*

A collection of spreads and instructions on how to get the most from them, the theory and practice of spread design, and tips to make your readings more useful.

Rachel Pollack's Tarot Wisdom

A fascinating journey through the tarot based on Rachel's lifetime of studies, explorations, and musings. Can be used with any tarot deck.

SUGGESTED READING

About the Artist

E ugene Smith lives and works in Chicago. He has a lovely wife and two daughters plus two not-so-terrible cats. He has been drawing all manner of strange things longer than he can remember.

Tell us a little about how you became an artist.

I have always loved to draw since I was a kid. It was just something I did for fun and enjoyment. It took me a while to realize I could make a living as an artist. I decided to take a leap and enrolled in the Academy of Art University in San Francisco. Going to art school doesn't really make you an "artist," but it certainly helps you gain the focus you need to realize your goals. The important thing is that I don't think there was one moment in time where I "became" an artist. It's just something I gradually came into through practice and diligence.

Did you have a process that you used for each card?
If so, what was that process?

Process is really important when creating illustrations. It starts with sketches, which help me think through the visual ideas I have in regards to the individual card. I use a lot of references pulled from the Internet for visual aids. I then take the sketch and create a more refined drawing using a light box. From there I scan in the drawing and color it in Photoshop, as well as add textural layers and effects to enhance the mood.

Was this your first experience with tarot? Did you
learn anything interesting? Was there anything
that surprised you?

I hadn't had any personal experience with tarot cards until I started this project. I didn't realize there was so much emphasis on symbols to prescribe meaning. I don't know why, and this is a little embarrassing to admit, but I think I always associated tarot cards with fortunetelling, which pretty much shows how little I knew about tarot. I was surprised to see it as a guide for understanding what's happening in the present. The complexity of the cards and the various permutations really reflect the complexity of life.

As an artist, how did you find the art for the original
Rider-Waite-Smith tarot? In what ways did it
inspire you? In what ways was it confining?

I found the RWS art very simple and direct. But I also feel that there is a wealth of detail and symbolic imagery. The one thing that I felt was confining was the use of composition

ABOUT THE ARTIST

in the pieces; sometimes the cards seemed to be more concerned with getting the symbols out there rather than using them in a visually appealing way. As a result the cards can feel cramped, and I think that can affect one's ability to fully take in the symbolic imagery.

What was your favorite image to work on and why?

I really loved working on the Death card. There is so much going on and it has a much more complex meaning than one would assume. I love the different reactions from the characters in the card—the way the young woman turns away in fear, the offering of flowers from the little girl, the stoic acceptance of the priest. It conveys a whole panoply of emotions in one image. It's also interesting in that it isn't literally about death but more about moving on from one thing to another, and that it can be seen as a good thing.

What was the most challenging and why?

The High Priestess card was the most challenging by far. I think that a lot of it has to do with a very specific feeling that needs to be conveyed from the character herself. The posture and emotion of the High Priestess character becomes a kind of symbol in itself, and that was very hard to pull off successfully. It took a lot of reworking to get the card to where it needed to be.

ABOUT THE ARTIST